MW01282261

BITE-SIZE
YOGA

A Better
Way to Beat
Burnout

NICOLE PAGE

Copyright © 2019 Nicole Page

All rights reserved.

No part of this book may be used or reproduced by any means, graphic, electronic, or mechanical, including photocopying, recording, taping or by any information storage retrieval system without the written permission of the author except in the case of brief quotations embodied in critical articles and reviews.

Because of the dynamic nature of the Internet, any web addresses or links contained in this book may have changed since publication and may no longer be valid.

The author of this book does not dispense medical advice or prescribe the use of any technique as a form of treatment for physical, emotional, or medical problems without the advice of a physician, either directly or indirectly. The intent of the author is only to offer information of a general nature to help you in your quest for emotional and spiritual well-being. In the event you use any of the information in this book for yourself, which is your constitutional right, the author assumes no responsibility for your actions.

Cover Photo by Megan Beck of New Earth Photo
(www.newearthphoto.net)

Author rev. date: 11/26/2019

ISBN: 9781077442085

FREE BOOK BONUSES

To say thank you for buying my book, I would like to gift you the MP3 meditations and PDF worksheets for the exercises in this book 100% for free! This way you can take your favorite meditations on-the-go with you whenever you need a Bite-Size Yoga break.

To download your free book bonuses, go to <u>www.beautifulsoulnicole.com/bite-size-yoga</u>.

DEDICATION

This book is dedicated to every person and experience along my path, whether challenging or beautiful, that has helped me grow and share this healing journey. I love and respect you as a part of myself.

CONTENTS

ACKNOWLEDGMENTS

Many people and schools have influenced this journey. In particular, I would like to recognize:

- Psychic Awakenings of Seattle, WA and Kimberly Sherry, International Energy Healer

- Casa Shipibo of Iquitos, Peru

- Shoshoni Yoga Ashram of Rollinsville, CO

- The Kirtan Leadership Institute of Boulder, CO

- Durga's Tiger School of Tumbaco, Ecuador

Also, I'd like to give a special thanks to the Self-Publishing School and Qat Wanders for helping me get this book out of my head and into the world!

INTRODUCTION

Hey There!

Do you wake up each day to the same old grind? You work to your limit and then crash as soon as you're done? You want a better work-life balance, but you've still got all those projects to finish?

Whether you're a professional, parent, or retiree, years of accumulated stress from overworking will take a toll on your health and, ultimately, your happiness. But you don't have the time to make a drastic lifestyle change.

What can you do right now, without sacrificing your output or your time, that will make your work habits more sustainable, and healthy, in the long run?

Let's Talk

I know burnout. Like you, I grew up trying to get past survival mode to become a blissfully productive member of society. I followed the conventional formula from college student to corporate worker for what was promised to be a happy and secure life. But the reality of this lifestyle was, honestly, soul-crushing.

Starting young, I packed my schedule with extracurriculars, volunteering, and internships to build the ideal resume. I got into an Ivy League college, studied abroad, and hoped to make the world a better place. When I graduated during the recession, there were few open doors. But, eventually, I clawed my way into the professional workforce.

Over time and a graduate degree later, I hit several professional pinnacles. I became a software developer through on-the-job training and then moved into corporate e-learning. I even passed the notorious Amazon HQ interviews to land a job at the corporate giant. Through some executive-level miscommunication, I ended up in recruiting instead of learning and development, but I had a safe, well-paid job.

All I had to do was show up every day for the rest of my life, and I would be set. But I was miserable.

This misery, from overworking and exhaustion, spilled into my personal life and relationships, making me sick. I became an alcoholic with an anxiety disorder. It wasn't worth it.

I, like everyone else, was promised that external success would be matched by internal fulfillment. But this wasn't the case for myself and many of my peers. I wanted to be successful and enjoy life, but I needed a new approach.

* * *

The Yoga Solution

I started learning yoga and meditation to find a better way to cope with stress and improve my work-life balance. While yoga routines were helpful in the studio, I needed a more applicable approach to take with me on-the-go.

That's when I started adding brief yogic activities into my day. First, I practiced mantra meditation in the morning before work. Then, I used breathing exercises in between meetings for a quick reset. My colleagues got used to seeing me do simple stretching routines at my desk, and, eventually, my anxiety attacks diminished, so I didn't have to call in sick as often.

Ultimately, I found stability and joy in my desk job by adding these Bite-Size Yoga breaks to my day. My coworkers and family started asking me about these techniques, so I threw off the chains of mediocre salaried security to become a yoga and meditation teacher!

Working with Others

First, I immersed myself in a yoga teacher training at an *ashram* or spiritual yoga center in the mountains of Colorado. Then I studied *kirtan*, the chanting and singing of Sanskrit mantra. During this time, I also trained as a professional energy healer, and later I explored shamanism and Kaula Tantra yoga in Latin America.

When I started teaching yoga classes, my students had the same challenges that I had initially experienced. They enjoyed yoga but felt like they were just following along in class. They wanted to be able to practice the techniques on their own and integrate them into their lives but didn't know how. Or worse, they wanted to try yoga to improve their health and anxiety but couldn't find the right classes for their level.

So, I geared my instruction towards sharing tricks and techniques that my students could take home with them. I encouraged personal internal exploration so they would feel empowered to mold their practice to meet their needs. In private sessions, I tailored activities beyond the usual yoga poses to achieve my students' personal goals, such as calmness and stability, through techniques like mantra, breath, and energy work.

But yoga classes and private sessions require the luxury of time and money, something I didn't have when entering the workforce. How do you get to a yoga class between errands, driving children around to their activities, or on a retirement budget? I realized there was a wider audience who needed these tools.

Making it Bite-Size

I wrote this book, and an accompanying online course, to distill the plethora of yoga practices into easy, fast, bite-size yoga techniques that anyone can add to their day. This way, without any previous experience and in just a short amount of time, you can bring more balance into your life and create long-term stress-relieving results.

This system of integrating yoga and meditation techniques into my day got me through my toughest times, and I hope it will work just as well for you. I call this system Bite-Size Yoga.

* * *

What is Bite-Size Yoga?

Bite-Size Yoga is when you use quick and easy yoga techniques to refresh your mind, body, and spirit whenever you start to feel your energy fading. Rather than propping yourself up on stimulants or working until you crash to get through your day, these techniques only take a few minutes and can be done anywhere. No yoga mat required.

Plus, you will never get bored because there are Bite-Size Yoga techniques for your breath, body, voice, mind, and spirit.

With Bite-Size Yoga, you can:

- Break the cycle of working and crashing.

- Create a new routine of working and refreshing with Bite-Size Yoga breaks!

How Does Bite-Size Yoga Improve Your Experience of Yoga Classes?

Your ability to enjoy yoga classes expands when paired with your daily Bite-Size Yoga practice. I've met so many students who say they've been to yoga classes, but they don't feel fluent in the tools and techniques of yoga because they feel like they're just playing a game of follow-the-yoga-instructor.

With Bite-Size Yoga, you develop a personal relationship with several different yoga practices, without having to invest the time or money in an intensive teacher training. Then, in yoga classes, you'll have a stronger foundation to connect with and modify the yoga postures that are thrown at you in quick succession. This new relationship empowers you to become more comfortable and fully present in your practice as well as easily extract your favorite techniques to reuse in your own Bite-Size Yoga routine!

How to Add Bite-Size Yoga to Your Day

In this book, I will teach you five Bite-Size Yoga techniques and lay out the system for how to make these incremental changes to your daily habits. This way, you won't have to trade your long-term health for short-term productivity.

* * *

There are Three Sections to this Book:

Section 1. The Work-Crash Cycle

Why you do so much, how you prop yourself up to get it all done, and why you can't stop doing it!

Section 2. Bite-Size Yoga

What is Bite-Size Yoga, and what are five techniques you can do right now to get instant relief from stress and fatigue?

Section 3. A Successful System

How to systematize your new Bite-Size Yoga habits into a daily routine for consistent results and easily organize your new techniques into a Bite-Size Yoga Toolkit for quick reference.

Plus, Extra Resources

Written instructions are helpful, but video demonstrations are always better! At the end of the book, there are even more resources to help you implement and grow your Bite-Size Yoga practice:

- The **Bite-Size Yoga Free Book Bonuses** online course provides video demonstrations and downloadable MP3s and PDFs for all the techniques taught in this book.

- The **Bite-Size Yoga 5-Week Online Boot Camp** is comprehensive online video course where, with the dedication of a simple daily schedule, you'll incrementally add five new Bite-Size Yoga techniques to your day for lasting results!

There is more information on these online resources at the end of the book, or you can jump to www.beautifulsoulnicole.com/bite-size-yoga to learn more now.

* * *

Are You Ready?

If you're sick of burnout and ready to revolutionize how you work, then this is the book for you. I'll see you in the first section where we'll look at the socially acceptable standard of working to your limit (and beyond) to see if there's a better way to meet your goals while supporting your health!

SECTION 1.

The Work-Crash Cycle

Are you tired of always working until you crash? Do you give it your all, until you feel like you have nothing left, and yet still feel unaccomplished or stressed? When your day is filled with working and crashing, and then, of course, working just a bit more, I call this the work-crash cycle. I was raised to believe this cycle is normal, but should it be?

By the end of this section, you'll be able to answer and reflect on these three questions:

1. Do you feel like you have to work until you crash?

2. Do you go through significant energy swings throughout your day?

3. Do you have any less-than-healthy habits that get you through your day, but are hard to let go of?

Are you ready to go from burned out to fired up? Let's get started!

CHAPTER 1.

A Daily Grind

Running on Empty

Rise and Shine

It's Monday morning. Your buzzer goes off on the bedside table next to your ear. You rub the crust from your eyes, squint at the light peeking through the blinds, and roll over for another snooze.

Eventually, you pry yourself from your cottony cocoon and walk like a zombie into the kitchen. You eat some food, down a cup of coffee or two, and slowly open your eyes to finally take a look around.

And You're Late!

The adrenaline pulses through your veins. With superhuman speed, you hop in and out of the shower, throw on some work clothes, and zip out the door, not totally sure whether you locked it or not.

Suddenly, you find yourself at your desk, sipping on your third or fourth cup of coffee, and BAM you are alive! But after a few hours of astonishing productivity, those heavy eyelids (and now sagging shoulders) are back with a vengeance.

You consider a few options:

1. **Pass out at your desk.** You might be able to squeeze in a quick nap, but you'll be in trouble if your boss comes around the corner.

2. **Load up on caffeine and cookies.** Sure, it comes with a crash, increased tension, and expanded waistline, but it'll buy you a few more hours, and at least it's legal.

3. **Ignore those signals of fatigue and just power through.** A little physical and emotional repression never hurt anyone, right?

And That's It!

You're out of options. Or at least you don't have the mental capacity to study up on any new mindfulness tricks, much less deal with your resistance to trying something new.

Oh yeah, and you needed immediate relief like two hours ago.

Then Your Coworker Brenda Walks By

You know the one who looks like she walked out of a health and fitness magazine? In the next cubicle over, she's talking about how amazing her 6:00 a.m. sunrise yoga made her feel as she sips her adaptogen-rich turmeric non-dairy latte with liquefied dandelion root.

You look down at your frosted jelly-filled donut with the bitter taste of motor-oil coffee still on your tongue and think, "That's nice, but who's got time for that?"

* * *

Working and Crashing

Sound familiar? That's what my typical workday used to look like – for real! Each day was a new cycle of too much to do and not enough time, or energy, to do it all.

Playing Catch-up

When I graduated from college at the end of 2009, still during the recession, the lack of entry-level professional jobs was depressing. I had to hustle to teach myself those on-the-job skills expected of mid-level employees and convince companies that I was qualified.

To cope with the pressure, push through rejection, and overcome slow learning curves, I fueled my day with caffeine, sugar, and nicotine. Then, after work, I drank away my stress with wine and beer to unwind and drown my discontent. By my mid-twenties, I was an alcoholic with an anxiety disorder and addicted to cigarettes.

That lifestyle, of pushing and propping myself up until I crashed, burned me out. Eventually, I would just quit whatever job I had, thinking that I was in the wrong industry. I told myself that it would be somehow different the next time around. But it never was.

I Wasn't Alone

As I moved around different companies and industries, I saw the same patterns in my peers. They were young professionals as well, working so hard to climb the corporate ladder while portraying a *Pinterest-perfect* lifestyle. By their late twenties, they were losing hair, breaking out in rashes, and medicating (or self-medicating) for stress disorders.

But this experience wasn't just limited to the twenty-somethings.

I watched as other co-workers, as well as family members, continued to let their health go in favor of professional and personal expectations. As they entered their 30s, 40s, and 50s, they had developed chronic anxiety and physical tension that impeded their quality of life and mental outlook.

By the time they reached their 60s, they had trouble contemplating retirement. They didn't know where to begin to undo the years of damage to their bodies and minds so they could actually relax and enjoy their hard-earned time off. They'd never known any other way to be.

* * *

Everyone's Got Too Much on Their Plates

These unrealistic demands on time and productivity aren't just limited to the workplace. They affect everyone. And each segment of society has its own challenges and expectations to manage on top of their already lengthy to-do lists.

Retirees

Just because you're retired doesn't mean life slows down. There is the bucket list of hobbies, adventures, and families to visit. And whether you like it or not, as you get older, your body may not have the same stamina or mobility it used to. Add on the stress of a fixed income life-style or reinventing your identity post-career (if you even stopped working at all) and pushing yourself until you crash, or get sick or injured, is just as much a reality as when you were younger.

Parents

Parents also have to meld their personal and professional responsibilities from before children with their new parental roles. I've heard from friends who, upon returning to work after starting a family, felt like they sucked at both their professional job and being a parent. They didn't have enough time or energy to do their best at everything. Yet they felt the pressure, and external scrutiny, to seem like they had it all together.

The List Goes On and On

Students have the weight of the world on their shoulders. They are trying to live up to their family's expectations, compete with their peers for limited spots on sports teams, cast lists, college admissions, job applications—all while trying to figure out their place in the world and who they really are.

Veterans returning from duty, and their families, have to reconcile their military experiences with home life, coping with any residual mental or physical wounds. Also, veterans may face societal judgment depending on the political climate they served in. They may also have to reinvent their role in the workforce, depending on whether they choose to continue with the military or start a civilian career (if they can work at all upon returning home).

Individuals with **mental health disorders or disabilities** and their families also deal with the same societal pressure to be high performers. On top of this pressure, they have the added complexity of managing their mental, physical, and familial situations. Trying to live up to intense productivity demands are potentially both physically and emotionally taxing, if attainable at all.

Professionals not only have demands at their workplace but also are expected to be available and potentially working at all hours of the day. Gone are the days of 9-to-5. Now, companies hand out work phones, virtual login portals, and work computers, so employees can be on call at any time without ever genuinely unplugging. How do you compete for a raise with your coworker who puts in eighty hours a week?

Even **hourly workers** might be emailed training to complete or be texted by their managers during inappropriate or un-clocked hours. Setting boundaries might cost them their jobs.

Entrepreneurs rarely take a break since any hour of the day is potentially a working hour of the day. Especially as they try to get their businesses off the ground and make a living, not responding to an email right away might cost them a sale. This lifestyle can hurt their families or prevent them from developing meaningful relationships outside of work.

Sometimes burnout is even a measure of success since it proves that you worked really, *really* hard.

* * *

Too Many Burners and Not Enough Gas

None of us live in a vacuum or can be put into a box. And yet the different aspects of our lives and all the associated demands on our time can leave us feeling fragmented and isolated as we manage our ever-evolving identities.

But trying to do too much is like lighting all the burners on your stove (and oven and broiler), without enough gas to keep them all going. Eventually, they'll all fizzle out, and you won't be able to cook anything!

* * *

Dog-Eat-Dog Expectations

Why Are Demands on Our Time So Extreme?

We live in a time that values immediate results over sustainability. Cultural competition is encouraged by reports of workforce scarcity. Plus, social media enables a means of instant comparison of your posted successes with those of your peers. You can never be good enough!

For example, throughout life, I've held and heard beliefs such as:

- **Work always comes first.** Your coworker stays at the office all night to get the next release finished. He never pushes back on requests. If another round of layoffs come, who do you think they'll keep?

- **Oh, and free time?** You should be learning new professional skills to make sure you get that 3% "exceeds expectations" raise on your next review. Otherwise, your salary will depreciate against annual inflation. But also cultivate a prestigious hobby, so you appear cultured and intriguing at networking events.

- **And did you see so-and-so's living room remodel?** It's so *Instagram-worthy*. I heard they did all the construction and design themselves. They should get a show on HGTV. They make it look so easy! I need to remodel my kitchen, so everyone knows I can do that, too.

These and many other commonly held societal values prioritize competition over a balanced lifestyle. But competition isn't all bad. It often drives self-improvement, which can be fulfilling and is essential to any healthy and progressive society.

But when oppressive professional demands and manufactured social media perfection become the ideal, individuals start sacrificing their long-term health to achieve unrealistic, and often unattainable, goals in the short term. This ticking time bomb will ultimately result in a sick workforce with low-morale.

Being overworked isn't just your problem, it's a systemic one.

* * *

What's Your Kryptonite?

Like Superman and his space rock, which kinds of demands leave you powerless to balance your priorities with self-care?

Maybe it's not corporate work, but family responsibilities, entrepreneurship, or academic pursuits that have you burning the candle at both ends. These obligations lead you to make lifestyle choices that prop you up in the short term but are detrimental to your long-term health and enjoyment of life.

Which demands keep taking precedence over your physical and mental well-being?

But What Can You Do?

Even if you can't change the system or the expectations of you as a professional, parent, or retiree, you *can* change how you operate within that system to create more balance, reduce stress, and still be productive.

In fact, if you learn how to balance self-care with productivity, in the long run, you may outpace your peers who have long since burned out!

So Why Don't You?

While more balance is the obvious solution, why isn't it the reality? In the next chapter, we'll cover the most common ways we manipulate time to live up to these extreme expectations and what is the price of this kind of schedule in the long run.

* * * * *

Chapter 1. Bite-Size Review

1. Often, when you work-till-you-crash, you have to prop yourself up with unhealthy short-term solutions to get results fast.

2. Over time, those habits become patterns that may lead to chronic illness and dissatisfaction, paving the road to burnout.

3. Everyone, from professionals to parents to retirees, feels the pressure of high expectations to get more done than is actually manageable in the time available.

4. Society encourages this imbalanced daily over-drive by pitting us against each other to achieve unrealistic professional and personal ideals as measures of self-worth and success.

5. Even if you can't change the system, you can change the way you operate within it to strike a balance between long-term health and short-term productivity.

CHAPTER 2.

Cutting Corners

Are You Ignoring Your Body's Signals?

When you're going through your day, do you ever start to get that crick in your neck? You know, the one from looking down at your phone, computer screen, or task list for too long? Maybe you unconsciously roll your shoulders or just give yourself a little rub, but mostly you press on without a second thought?

At the end of the day, week, month, years, etc., the pain has escalated to needing medication, a chiropractor, or potentially has re-sculpted your spine (and not for the better). But at least you got your work done, right?

For me, I go into autopilot when writing at my desk. I want to bang out another blog post, chapter, or course script. Often, I'm tempted to power through until I finish *just one more* page before I take a break for some necessary self-care. I know full well that once I do conclude that page, paragraph, or post, I will make another excuse to keep working, always promising my body I'll step away soon but never actually fulfilling that promise.

In the meantime, my hips ache and my mouth is dehydrated. The other chores I need to get done are weighing on my mind. My breathing becomes erratic as my mind starts to worry about whether I'll get everything done. But I just keep sitting at my desk, trying to work through the worsening signals.

This is not productive for my current project or my health. And rather than work through my fractured attention, I could've just taken a few minutes to stretch. I even could've thrown a load of laundry in the washer. Then, I would've returned to my desk with a clear mind and fewer distractions. But I fell prey to the "just... one... more..." monster.

The "Just... One... More..." Monster

Your body doesn't mess around. It lets you know when it needs to rest and reset for optimal performance. But do you listen? Or are you trying to get through "just one more" task before you take a break? Once this last item is complete, you tell yourself you'll be more than ready to give your body and mind the attention and care they crave.

But will you?

If you weren't responding to your body's demand for attention in the first place, do you really think you'd prioritize it later? Or is it likely that another project, unplanned request, or forgotten time-sensitive task will rise to the forefront once you finish that "just one more" thing?

And why would you take a break? If you can push through and get "just one more" thing done today, then you won't have to keep track of it tomorrow!

You plan to get that rest back when you go to bed, but you have trouble sleeping. You've trained your mind to always be going, and you don't quite have the skills to quiet it. So, you binge-watch TV until you can barely lift yourself from the couch.

When your alarm goes off the next morning, you're groggy and drained. But you get up and start the cycle all over again.

* * *

Borrowing on Credit

When you try to do more than your natural cycle allows, you have to manipulate your energy to get it all done. But there are consequences for this borrowed surge. At some point, your body will override your will and forcefully reclaim the energy it's due.

And you crash.

How Does This Happen?

There is a lot of pressure to get more done in a day than is reasonably possible. When I sit down to write out what I think will be a to-do list for the day, more often than not, it ends up being more realistically a to-do list for the week. Yet, even with this awareness, I put so much pressure on myself to try to get it all done in a day, and then I mentally beat myself up when I don't.

Where Do Your Expectations or To-Do Lists Go Overboard?

Think you can knock out that bathroom remodel in a weekend? Get the perfect report to your boss in an hour? Finish that book by the end of the week? To accomplish the impossible, you have to get more productive with the time you've got.

The Art of Manipulation

There are two factors you can manipulate to try to get more done in a day: time and energy.

Time

The number of hours in a day is fixed, so you can't change that. But what you do with your time is under your control.

For example, you could find new ways to streamline and simplify your habits to make yourself more efficient and ultimately save time. But all that research, testing, and learning curves take time! Precisely what you don't have enough of.

You tell yourself, eventually you'll look into a new energy-boosting smoothie or learn to meditate, but for the moment you've got 10 other things that need to get done, and you need results right now!

Energy

The other factor you have a little more control over is your energy. So, what might a healthy energy cycle look like?

Well, throughout the day, your body goes through several work-and-rest rhythms:

1. **Deep Rest:** You wake up from your overnight sleep.

2. **Work:** You want to get things done, so you work until your energy depletes.

3. **Rest:** You need to rest and refuel again. So, you eat, move, or take a break until you feel refreshed.

4. **Work:** You work some more for as long as you have the energy to focus.

5. **Rest:** You take another break to refresh.

6. **Repeat:** And so, the cycle continues until you're ready for bed to take another deep rest, fully restoring your energy for the next day.

It's a pretty simple cycle. But when a deadline is looming, we start to cut corners. And often that first corner is rest.

* * *

Who Has Time to Rest?

Do you need to shop, cook, and clean for your family? Don't forget nurturing your friendships and career! And have you made any headway on that DIY headboard you found on Pinterest yet? With all these competing priorities, you may start to wonder, "Do I really need to rest?"

It's tempting. If you cut out rest, you have more work time.

How Do You Cut Out Rest?

When you skip your rest rhythm in favor of getting more things done, you have to summon that energy from something else.

The most straightforward and accessible ways to skip rest are:

1. To artificially boost your energy with stimulants, so you can go just a little longer.

2. To ignore the signals of fatigue and power on through sheer determination.

What's your go-to trick when you need to push through your day without taking any breaks?

Benefits: You Get More Done...

When you cut out rest, in the short term, you win!

You hit a few more stops on your errands route, you knock out a few more chapters in your book, and you proudly tick off the most boxes at your team's next status meeting.

But at what cost?

...Then You Crash

You may get a few more tasks crossed off your list when you cut out rest at first. But eventually, you will crash from pushing your body, and your brain, into overdrive.

Crashing is when your body and nervous system override your desire to be active and productive. Your eyes force themselves shut and you have to pay back the borrowed time, of skipping rest, with interest. You may even require more rest than you previously needed to get back to a balanced state.

* * *

Your Balance is Past Due

When you cut out rest from your natural work-rest cycle, it becomes a work-crash cycle:

1. **Deep Rest:** Wake up refreshed from sleep.

2. **Work:** Work until your energy depletes.

3. **Work:** Work through the depletion, by propping yourself up with stimulants or ignoring fatigue, until your second dip in energy. Your mind is a little less efficient, but you're still making progress.

4. **Work:** Keep pushing through, you're almost there! Maybe a quick walk to get just one more

coffee. It's not your best work, but that inbox is getting shorter.

5. **Crash:** Your body says, "No more!" and your mind shuts down. You get home just in time to order takeout, crack open a beer, and zone out for the next four hours.

6. **Mediocre Rest:** Eventually, you get ready for bed, but you have a hard time getting to sleep because your cycle is off. You scroll through your phone until you finally pass out. When you wake up the next day, you don't feel refreshed, but you press on.

In the short term, you technically get more done. But, as your energy wanes, the quality of your work decreases until finally your mind and body take over with a complete system shut down. And depending on how long you pushed yourself past your energetic expiration, you might not fully recover by the next day, leaving you groggy and not performing at your best.

You tell yourself that you'll just catch up on sleep over the weekend to balance things out. But is it enough?

* * *

The Long-Term Costs of Overriding Natural Cycles

Even though you say you'll eventually work on better habits, eventually doesn't always come. That same to-do list that caused you to cut corners in the first place has already refilled itself (and then some) by the time you've woken up the next morning.

So, you keep pushing through your fatigue for days, weeks, maybe even years. Sure, there are a few hard crashes where you're knocked out for a few days by a weakened immune system or just pure exhaustion, but you keep returning to the same habits. You feel like you always have to be "on."

But what does that do to your health?

A Body That Can't Keep Up

Your body has this miraculous ability to regenerate tissue and self-heal. But what you feel as emotional stress when you work, also causes physical stress in the body that your immune system needs to tend to. When you take away the time your body used to use to heal itself, your body's to-do list also builds up.

Now, your body has the same problem that you do - too much to do and too little time to do it! More work time for you equals less work time for your body. And just as the quality of your work decreases when you work on borrowed energy, so does your body's immune system.

In fact, your body's workers may not even get to maintaining some of their central systems because they're so busy coping with the inflammatory stimulants you ingested, the excess adrenaline from stress, and the aching weakening muscles from your seated marathons behind your desk. Over time, your body just can't keep up, and you might get sick or even develop chronic issues that require medical intervention.

A Lower Quality of Life

And let's face it. When your body feels like crap, you feel like crap. You can't move through the world with the same joy because you're constantly bombarded with stings of pain and tension. You may even hit a physical or emotional rock bottom.

Then, the symptoms of your overworking are so well-established that, even with a restful vacation or therapeutic intervention, your body doesn't quickly bounce back. And if you do commit to a new lifestyle, because of the backlog of issues you've been accumulating over the years, the results and relief won't be immediate. You're stuck finally paying for all the short-cuts you took before.

Running Out of Options

So, what can you do? You still don't have the time or energy to make drastic life changes right now, like 5:00 a.m. yoga or a restriction diet. There has to be a way to integrate self-care to support or even improve your daily productivity while also getting the energetic refreshment you need.

The key to not needing serious intervention or completely uprooting your lifestyle is to make small changes to your daily habits before the symptoms of overwork become catastrophic.

Easier Said Than Done

If the solution to creating more balance is as easy as making small changes, why isn't this the norm? What's stopping you from making even just a little time for self-care in your day?

In the next chapter, we'll cover why you might not have made the lifestyle adjustments you know you should've made and what you need to know so that you can successfully make those changes.

* * * * *

Chapter 2. Bite-Size Review

1. The "Just... One... More..." monster keeps you from listening to your body's signals to take a break.

2. When you're trying to increase how much you get done in a day, the main factors you are able to manipulate are time and energy.

3. Your body naturally moves through rhythms of work and rest. When you cut out rest, in the short term you get more time, but it's like borrowing energy on credit. Eventually, your body has to collect the energy it's due, and it crashes when you default on your promise to rest up.

4. Cutting out rest in the long-term leads to chronic issues when your body can't keep up with its daily maintenance tasks. Then, when your body feels bad, you feel bad, and your quality of life starts to go downhill.

5. If you wait until physical conditions become catastrophic before you make a change, you will need a radical lifestyle intervention, which you still may or may not have the time, or will, for.

6. The key to not making drastic changes but still promoting a healthy and productive lifestyle is to make small changes to your workflow before your symptoms of exhaustion become severe.

NICOLE PAGE

CHAPTER 3.

Broken Habits

Are You Blinded?

You're smart. I bet you already know which habits of yours are and aren't good for you. Yet you keep going back to them, day after day. Why is that?

It's Because You're in Love.

You're in love with the results you get from those habits. Maybe those results are a feeling of accomplishment or a surge of energy from that coffee or donut. You receive that rewarding feeling once and logically you equate, "If I keep doing that thing, I'll keep getting that reward."

Over time, this type of love become dependence.

An Addictive Personality

I've always known that I have an easily addictive personality. When I was young, if I found an activity that gave me a thrill, I would obsessively pursue it until I lost interest. In high school, I would look up colleges and majors all over the world for hours, day-dreaming about all the lives I could lead. As I got older, and my access to less innocent activities increased, I latched onto coffee, cigarettes, and alcohol, looking to those rushes of chemical reactions to bring me pleasure.

My peers managed these same stimulants with moderation, but I never could. When I smoked, I was a chain-smoker. When I drank alcohol, it was wine by the bottle. A "moderate" day of coffee for me was three to five cups.

Another Refill Please

Trying to understand my addictions, I watched a documentary on alcoholism (reference unknown). In this film, there was a medical study recorded where someone could indicate that they would like more alcohol and the nurse would administer it in doses via an I.V. Not exactly a bar scene, but the test was to see when different people would stop asking for more alcohol.

The expectation was that a "normal person" would at some point notice that the balance of pleasant to unpleasant side-effects of alcohol would change, and they would stop requesting more. However, someone with an "overactive reward center" would never feel like the unpleasant side-effects overcame the rush of pleasant ones. The reward center in their brain always communicated that more was a good idea, and as long as the person was allowed a choice, they would keep picking yes.

An Overactive Reward Center

This concept of an overactive reward center helped me understand a lot about my compulsive behavior, whether it was with alcohol, coffee, or just staying up all night to play Pokémon on old Gameboys. Even though I was getting some signals to stop, I had such a hard time passing up just one more round of... *whatever*, because it always felt so good.

Eventually, my body would shut down anyway by either crashing, passing out, or blacking out. Yet I still wasn't motivated enough to change my actions.

Addicted to Results

It might seem like substance addiction is a far departure from unhealthy work habits, but it was those same compulsions that propped up my work-crash habits as I ignored signals of fatigue with feel-good stimulants.

While alcohol and cigarettes may not be your poison, there is some reason you forgo healthy long-term habits during your work day in favor of these quick fixes and shortcuts to get more done. You've become reliant upon the rewards and results of working until you crash, even though you know it's not good for you long-term.

* * *

Breaking Dependency

If you're doing something that you know isn't good for you in the long run, but you keep doing it anyway, because of the results it produces, you've become dependent. Your will is being overpowered by the reward. Sometimes you make it through periods of healthier choices, but ultimately, you keep falling back on your old tricks. Why?

There's No Time

The universe loves a void. Why? Because it will fill it!

As soon as you make space in your calendar to research some new productivity or self-care habits, in comes a new slew of tasks, requests, and chores that need addressing. What little mental capacity you had available is now being spent trying to prioritize those.

With the best intentions, you try to chip away at a few quick tasks. Before you know it, you're back in the flow of work, without even having gotten a chance to rest or make a change.

Changing habits costs time, the very thing that led you to cut corners in the first place. To change habits, first you have to:

1. Research new ones.

2. Test them out to see if they work for you.

3. Persevere through learning curves, which mean slower results, as you get up to speed.

This is a lengthy process. You have to sacrifice the time you could've spent getting your regular immediate results because you believe this investment will pay you back with more efficiency and sustainability in the long-term. But it's a risk. And you're not always willing or feel like you can afford to take that risk.

Results Not Guaranteed

Especially with lifestyle changes, there's no guarantee that someone's blog post about what got them better results will work equally well for you. This is why some people will hire someone one-on-one, to identify and teach them what exactly they need to do to bridge their performance gaps. But they've still got to follow-through on what they're taught.

You can hire the best coaches and trainers money can buy, but if you don't commit to a systemic change to your lifestyle (even just a small one), your results will be as temporary as your payroll.

Letting Go

Even if you do overcome the barrier to learn something new, you still have to let go of the habit that doesn't serve you. It doesn't matter how many yoga classes you attend if you refill your body with cocktails (or your not-so-healthy product of choice) at the end of each night, because your liver and organs never really detox.

* * *

Why Is It So Hard to Say Goodbye?

It's a Little Emotional

When I reach for my first coffee of the day, it makes me feel like a million bucks. I'm clear-minded, I'm confident, and I'm energized enough to save the world! Each time I take a sip, I reconnect to that image of fearlessness and power, reinforcing the Pavlovian response (coffee = invincibility).

Eventually, though, I get tired. I keep refilling my cup, impatiently trying to re-awaken that superhuman strength, but nothing changes. I am probably just dehydrated. Yet, just like the definition of insanity, I keep repeating the same action (drinking more coffee) expecting a different result.

In fact, it's worse than that. I consciously acknowledge that if I drink a coffee in the afternoon, I will pass out almost immediately in an instant crash. Yet I try it anyway, thinking that "maybe this time" it'll work. Not good.

I clearly have an emotional association with this habit that overrides all logical reasoning. It's like staying on the couch, eating popcorn, and letting your eyes glaze over as you watch TV. You know you'd be better off just going to bed, but there is a sense of comfort from the salty carbs and losing yourself in passive entertainment that overrides your rational mind.

When it comes to changing habits, there is an underlying fear that if you let go of that external habit, you may also lose the inner feeling of joy, confidence, etc., that it creates.

And a Little Physical

In addition to the emotional dependency you have on your *less-than-healthy* habits, you may also have a physical one. Many stimulants that help you override the desire to rest are addictive. Sugar and carbs leave you craving more sugar and carbs. If you stop feeding your caffeine monster, you may get severe headaches from withdrawal. And quitting smoking is so challenging because of the nicotine that it has its own industry.

Even if your crutch isn't addictive, you train your body to expect a specific input at a particular time of day. Your body automatically reaches for it, and if that craving isn't fulfilled, you may become irritable.

But It's Not Impossible

The physical and emotional coping mechanisms that get you through your day are so ingrained, that, even if you knew what you should replace them with, they can be hard to let go of. But swapping out less healthy habits for better ones doesn't have to be so hard. You just have to find new means for the same ends.

* * *

Habit Swapping

A New Means to an End

The process of breaking your corner-cutting habits is pretty simple to describe, but harder to achieve. If you're daring enough to make a change:

1. Figure out what need is being met by your current habit.

2. Identify something healthier that meets that same need.

3. Swap the habits so you can still fulfill your need while also supporting your health.

If you know what you're trying to achieve with your old habit, you just need to find a new means to the same end. This way, you get your reward (for example the feeling of invincibility) without the previous consequences (like crashing or chronic issues due too many cups of coffee).

Adjusting Expectations

It's important to acknowledge that your new habit may not be as effective or as intense as your original crutch.

For example, with my overactive reward center, alcohol literally made me feel bliss. This created a tall order to find a suitable alternative through more natural means. I even failed at sobriety twice before finally finding the right balance on the third try.

Sugar and coffee are called stimulants for a reason. They get you from zero-to-sixty fast. It's hard to find an alternative or activity that packs the same punch as refined sugar that is also healthy for you and not prone to abuse.

Your new habit may not match your old one in intensity, but it has to get you most of the way to your first experience so that your craving feels satisfied. Then you can ultimately close that gap with the other long-term benefits of your new habit such as improved natural energy, physical health, and emotional well-being. But those long-term benefits only come along if you stick with it!

* * *

How to Make It Stick

You've got your new habit, and you're prepared for the bumps as you shift your perspective towards longer-term gains. How do you keep it up?

1. Your new habit needs to be reliable and reasonable.

2. You've got to practice it until it becomes automatic.

A Good New Habit

If you want to lower your risk of failure, you need a habit that is reliable and reasonable.

It Gives You Reliable Results

A reliable habit gets you to your intended result immediately. Even if the progress is incremental, there needs to be enough of a result to motivate you to continue. If you don't get results fast, you'll go back to what you know and have to pay for it later.

It's Reasonably Convenient. . .

A reasonable habit is something that you can actually do when you need it. A yoga class may guarantee to help you to reduce stress and refresh your energy, but if you can't swap your midday coffee with it, then it's not a reasonable replacement for this habit.

. . . And It's Reasonably Easy

If part of your resistance to change is that you don't have enough time to make healthier choices, then picking a new habit that is complicated or has a lot of rules won't last long.

There is always some on-boarding time for any new habit or system. But ultimately your habit needs to be as easy as possible so that you don't waste time trying to figure it out.

One of the reasons I always gave up on complicated elimination diets, even though they made me feel better, was because they took so much time to prep for. I had to plan out every single nutrient that would go into my body throughout the day, so I would be prepared whenever hunger struck. I had the stamina for this degree of preparation for a few days, but eventually, it was dinner time, I was tired, and a box of mac and cheese looked really easy.

Your new habit should be as convenient and straightforward as getting a bag of chips from the vending machine. Because, in the heat of the moment, you're not going to have a lot of time, or willpower, to make the choice that sacrifices instant gratification for long-term sustainability unless it's easy and, to some degree, pleasant.

Make It Automatic

The most natural habits are the ones you do automatically. You spend little to no brain power evaluating how you will tie your shoes today. You just do it. You may not even remember that you did. It was that automatic.

This is where your current work habits live. The patterns that involuntarily suppress your body's signals for rest are, at this point, automatic. You may not even be aware of them as they happen. Getting up to refill your coffee is just part of your routine whether you need it or not.

This means that it will take some effort and awareness to stop the original habits. But ideally, you want to get your new practices to the point where they too become a reflex. If taking a break to focus on your breath between meetings is just part of your routine, you aren't wasting energy, deciding what to do and how to do it each time you feel tired.

To make your new habits automatic, you have to practice them before you need them. If you get through the struggles of a learning curve and resistance to change when you're not under pressure, you'll more successfully be able to switch to those new habits when you need results fast.

If you don't make your new habits just as automatic as your old ones, you might not even remember the new tools you have and fall back on the slippery slope of your old habits and dependencies in the heat of the moment.

* * *

Finding a Unicorn

You may be wondering where do you find this unicorn that breaks the work-crash cycle but also helps you meet the practical needs of a full day?

If you haven't guessed yet from the title of this book, Bite-Size Yoga might just be the secret sauce that helps you get through the day, satisfying both your body's need to rest and your mind's desire to stay sharp and productive.

In the next section, we'll dive into Bite-Size Yoga and learn five simple techniques to start beating those burn-out blues (and temptations) today.

* * * * *

Chapter 3. Bite-Size Review

1. Your love affair with the rewards you get from less healthy habits, keeps you coming back for more, even when you know they're not good for you.

2. It's challenging to break your dependence on corner-cutting habits because:

    a. You don't have the time to invest in learning something new.

    b. You've become emotionally dependent on the habits you have.

3. You may even be physically dependent on your old habits.

4. To change your quick-fix habits, you have to swap them with new practices that meet the same needs.

5. To minimize the risk of failure, these new habits need to be reliable, convenient, and easy so that you still get some immediate results with the least amount of resistance.

6. You also need to practice these new habits before you need them, so they have a chance to become just as automatic and ready-to-use as your outdated crutches.

Section 1. Bite-Size Review

Wow! We've come so far in looking at how we manage our energy, why we put so much pressure on ourselves to get so much done, and how we manipulate our resources to try to get it all done. Let's take a moment to review what we've covered:

1. We're all running on empty as we try to feed the insatiable machine of social and economic competition.

2. Propping yourself up with instantly gratifying, yet unsustainable, habits to get just one more hour of productivity ultimately leads to devastating crashes and poor long-term health.

3. To successfully replace your unhealthier habits, you have to consider whether there might be another means to get to the same end.

There's another means to a sharp mind and physical stamina than another coffee? In the next section, we'll see that all is not lost in finding new tools that support both our productivity and our health.

Let's try out some Bite-Size Yoga!

SECTION 2.

BITE-SIZE YOGA

So, we've covered what isn't working in the current work cycle and massive projected expectations. How about some new options? Are there really yoga practices that you can do at the office or on the bus without getting stared at like a looney?

Now it's time to dive into some bite-size solutions to your big health and productivity problems! By the end of this section, you'll be able to answer and reflect on these three questions:

1. What is Bite-Size Yoga, and how do the five different flavors of Bite-Size Yoga techniques address your different tensions throughout the day?

2. How does Bite-Size Yoga conveniently balance your body's need for rest and your personal need for productivity?

3. What are five Bite-Size Yoga techniques that you can add to your day right now?

If you're ready to put down the coffee cup (well at least that afternoon refill) and summon your natural energy from within, then it's time to taste-test some Bite-Size Yoga!

Special Note: Video demonstrations of and downloadable resources for all the techniques in this section can be found at www.beautifulsoulnicole.com/bite-size-yoga under **Bite-Size Yoga Free Book Bonuses**.

CHAPTER 4.

A Bite-Size Solution

What Do You Picture When You Think of Yoga?

Is it chiseled bodies contorted into acrobatic positions? Or maybe it's wise, wrinkled faces meditating on mountain tops, reflecting on a lifetime of study and dedication? Perhaps it's a group of people sweating together in a hot studio following a drill sergeant instructor?

But do you know what's wrong with these images?

Unless you're a fitness influencer or an athlete paid to travel the world, they don't easily fit into an average day.

Sure, you might get in a yoga class or hike to a nearby rock face during the week. But all these associations portray yoga as a leisure activity. You have to have the luxury of time to fit it into your schedule, and you have to go somewhere special to do it.

Yoga Comes from Within

Yoga is not doing a series of poses in a class or sitting in meditation for hours on end. Those are tools of yoga, but they are not *yoga*.

Yoga is a state of unity from within. Yoga in Sanskrit (an ancient Indo-European language) means "to yoke" or "to join," as in yoking two oxen, so they can work together in unison. Yoga is the act of joining all aspects of yourself (mind, body, and spirit) so you can feel unified and complete, just as you are, at this moment.

Yoga is Meant to be Lived

Yoga is a philosophical system that provides tools for achieving this state of unity within yourself. This philosophy is meant to be lived so that you are always operating from a place of inner and outer harmony. And isn't this balance precisely what you're looking for in your workday?

* * *

Adding Yoga to Your Work Cycle

When you achieve balance in your yoga practice, you feel relaxed and alert. This state is also the optimal condition for a productive and healthy workday.

The Optimal "Flow" State

Flow is a term for when you are so fully engaged with the task-at-hand that you don't notice the time pass or get weary. You are wholly present and meditatively honed in on your project. You're in the zone.

Flow doesn't wear you down as much as grunting through your work because it's the right balance of challenging but achievable to keep you focused without feeling overwhelmed. It's the ideal work state.

Flow Through Work with Yoga

What if you could prime yourself to find flow in your workday by taking **quick yoga breaks** whenever your energy starts to wane or you lose your current momentum? This process would create a new work cycle of:

1. **Deep Rest:** You wake up from your nightly sleep.

2. **Work:** You get things done until you're depleted.

3. **Yoga Break:** When you need to rest and refuel, you do yoga to bring your awareness inward and recharge your mind, body, and spirit.

4. **Work:** You work some more until your energy wanes again.

5. **Yoga Break:** You take another yoga break to refresh.

6. **Repeat Until Sleep:** And so, the cycle continues until you're ready for bed and deep rest to restore your energy for the next day.

When you add yoga to your work-rest cycle, your energy rhythms never get thrown too far off towards exhaustion. Plus, you're motivated to take your yoga breaks because they help you create the optimal conditions for flow in your workday.

So how do you make yoga quick and portable so that you can practice it whenever and wherever you need to refresh your energy?

* * *

Make it Bite-Size

Bite-Size Yoga

Bite-Size Yoga is just a single yoga technique (or collection of techniques) that you can do anywhere from five to

10 minutes wherever you are. **No mat or yoga pants required.**

And you can organize this collection of techniques in, what I call, your **Bite-Size Yoga Toolkit**. A Bite-Size Yoga Toolkit is just an organizational system for tracking and storing the Bite-Size Yoga techniques you most enjoy based on what kind of yogic activity they belong to and what issues they best address.

What's in Your Bite-Size Yoga Toolkit?

Since yoga is a system for finding inner unity and balance within this system, there are many approaches to achieve this desired state.

For example, you can do:

- Breathing exercises (*pranayama*),

- Physical postures (*asana*),

- Chanting (*mantra*),

- Philosophical study (*jnana*),

- And meditation (*dhyana*) to name a few.

Don't worry if most of these Sanskrit names or practices aren't familiar to you. In the following chapters, we'll deep dive into each of these styles, exploring how they're relevant to your life and how to do them.

But in the meantime, to help you conceptualize how all of these practices fit into the yoga puzzle, I find it easier to group these different practices by which part of yourself they engage:

- *Pranayama* engages your **breath**.

- *Asana* engages your **body**.

- *Mantra* engages your **voice**.

- *Jnana* engages your **mind**.

- *Dhyana* engages your **spirit**.

Rather than worry about the Sanskrit term or yoga jargon, the techniques in your Bite-Size Yoga Toolkit can, therefore, be intuitively grouped by breath, body, voice, mind, or spirit.

I call these the five flavors of Bite-Size Yoga!

* * *

The 5 Flavors of Bite-Size Yoga

When Would You Use Which Flavor?

When it comes to picking the right tool for the job, usually I'd say to trust whichever technique comes to mind at that moment. But while you're still getting acquainted with how the different yoga techniques work for you, here's a general idea of what various stresses each flavor of yoga is most suited to address:

- Use techniques for the **breath** when you need to calm your nervous system.

- Use techniques for the **body** when you need to release physical strain and tension.

- Use techniques for the **voice** (or chant silently in your head) when you need to stop cycles of negative thoughts.

- Use techniques for the **mind** when you need to replace destructive beliefs with constructive ones.

- Use techniques for the **spirit** when you feel stuck and need to reconnect with your inner clarity.

These techniques not only address tensions that may accumulate throughout your day in your mind, body, and spirit, but they also draw your attention back inward. By removing your focus from the external events around you, over which you have no control, you put that energy into finding harmony and energetic refreshment within. In this way, you rest and reset in just a matter of minutes (or however much time you have) so that you can get back to your to-do list without sacrificing your health or quality of life.

* * *

Are You Ready to Taste Test Some Bite-Size Yoga Techniques?

Don't get stuck in analysis paralysis. Yoga is meant to be experienced, and you need tools you can use right now! In the next five chapters, you will learn a technique for each of the five flavors of Bite-Size Yoga as well as when and why to use it.

Be sure to try out each technique, even if you're not familiar with it or aren't sure whether you're doing it right. We all have different preferences. Some flavors of yoga may resonate more with you than others, and that's important to know as well because, if you want to strike a new balance between health and productivity in your life, you've got to try new things!

* * * * *

Chapter 4. Bite-Size Review

1. Yoga isn't something you do on a mountaintop or in a studio class, but a quality of complete unity you develop from within as you bridge the divisions of your mind, body, and spirit.

2. A yoga practice leaves you relaxed and alert, which is the optimal state for being productive and achieving flow in your daily activities.

3. Bite-Size Yoga is a collection of specific techniques you can insert into your day whenever you need a break to refresh your energy.

4. Bite-Size Yoga comes in five flavors of techniques based on whether they engage your breath, body, voice, mind, or spirit.

5. The five flavors of Bite-Size Yoga alleviate different kinds of stresses or tensions you might accumulate throughout your day, making them a healthy and effective way to regulate your energy and stay productive throughout your day.

CHAPTER 5.

Technique #1
Bite-Size Yoga
for Your Breath

Introduction

The Breath in Yoga

Yoga that focuses on your breath is called *pranayama*, or breathing exercises. In yoga philosophy, animating life force energy, or *prana*, is carried throughout your body on the breath.

No More Breath, No More Life

Think of your breath like an energetic circulatory system. In yoga, if your breathing is shallow or irregular, then your prana isn't circulating properly. If prana is blocked, then that physical area may become unwell because it is not getting the energy it needs to function correctly. Therefore, breath is necessary not only for keeping your body alive but also for sustaining energy for your spirit.

Why Should You Care?

Your quality of breath reflects the state of your nervous system.

When I first went to see a therapist about my anxiety, he asked me to start noticing my breath. He told me to pay attention to when I started holding my breath as a sign of rising tension because:

1. If I continued to hold my breath, then I might trigger a panic attack.

2. If I managed to regulate my breath as soon as I noticed the irregular breathing, then I would have a better chance of preventing a panic attack and calming down on my own.

Your breath reflects the state of your nervous system:

- If it's steady and calm, so are you.

- If it's all over the place, then your nerves are bouncing around as well.

If you can control your breath, then you can control your nervous system.

Yoga Helps You Breathe

There are many pranayama breathing exercises in yoga.

If you want to regulate your breath, yoga has a technique for every purpose. There are warming breaths and cooling breaths. There are exercises for breath lengthening, breath strengthening, breath awareness, etc. Even the asana practice of postures has specific breaths for each movement.

When you practice breathing, you practice regulating your nervous system. And if you can get through a full yoga practice with proper breathing, then you are training yourself to handle other life situations with steady breath as well as steady nerves.

But you don't have to go to a studio class or manipulate your breath like an abdominal contortionist to start practicing pranayama.

Anyone Can Breathe

When I moved cross-country with my ex-husband to Michigan from Seattle, we lived with his family for a few months while looking for a house. I was still working remotely for my Seattle company, while my former husband and his father would go to work. So, during the day, it was me, his retired mother, and the rescue dog.

My ex-mother-in-law was just a year into her retirement, but she still had trouble with all the accumulated anxiety from decades of raising a family and working. Even though it was subsiding, she still wasn't as relaxed as she could be while going about her day, taking care of the home, errands, family, and dog.

So, I asked if she wanted to do pranayama with me in the morning. After everyone else had left for work, we'd sit at the kitchen table and, for 15 minutes, I'd lead a simple breathing exercise. Afterward, we'd reflect on how the practice went and how it affected the rest of the day. We did this practice together for several months, and later, she still continued it on her own whenever she wanted to rest and reset.

* * *

Technique #1 the 100-Count Breath

This first Bite-Size Yoga technique I'm going to teach you is as easy as counting!

There are a lot of breath counting exercises, but I especially like this one because it makes the meditation a game by giving you a goal.

Honestly, this is probably not a traditional yoga practice. But yoga philosophy states that any activity that brings you closer to achieving inner union is a legitimate yoga practice. So, since you're a modern yogi, practicing in a contemporary context (such as your office, home, parking lot, etc...), this 100-count breath is a great place to start!

When to Use:

Use this technique whenever you're becoming agitated or holding your breath. This exercise is also suitable for setting a calm baseline for your day, especially if you tend to wake up a little stressed in the morning.

Instructions:

Step 1. Find a Seat

Find a comfortable seat so that your spine is long and straight, and your shoulders are relaxed. Breathe through your nose, if you can. Bring your attention to your breath.

Step 2. Start Counting on the Exhale

Take a deep inhale. Then as you exhale, count silently in your head, "One."

Step 3. Increment Your Count with Each Exhale

Increase the count with each round of breath so that on your next exhale you count two, then three, and so on.

Step 4. If You Forget What Number You're On, Start Over

This practice trains your breath and focus. If your mind starts to wander and you forget what number you're on, start over at one.

Step 5. Keeping Counting Until You Reach 100 (or Some Multiple of 100)

Keep counting your breath until you reach 100 breaths.

However, especially in the beginning, you may lose count frequently and have to start over a lot. Therefore, I recommend starting with a goal of 25 breaths. Then when that becomes consistent, increase the count up to 50, then 75, and finally 100.

Once you can keep your focus for a full 100 hundred breaths, the practice should only take about five to 10 minutes. But if you have only limited time available, set a timer and see how far you can get.

A focused breath practice, even for just five minutes, is enough to draw your energy and awareness inward so you can reset your nervous system. Then, when you return to your daily duties, you'll be a little more rested and relaxed than you were before!

* * *

Your Turn

Practice makes progress. If you want to replace your current coping habits with new skills, then you need to practice. The more you practice a new technique, the more quickly you'll be able to remember it when you're stressed and need it most.

Pro Tip

When regulating your breath, don't forget to breathe!

If you're supposed to breathe through your nose but your nose is stuffed, breathe through your mouth. Your ability to safely breathe and get oxygen always wins over the directions of a breathing exercise.

Alternatively, if you start feeling dizzy, stop the practice and return to your natural breath! There's a reason it's called a breathing exercise. You wouldn't do a marathon without training. Start with accessible practices and build from there.

What's Next?

You can either:

1. Take a few days to fully explore this technique (reflecting on your experiences in the notes space provided on the next few pages), or

2. Review all the exercises at once and just play with them as you go.

You are building a Bite-Size Yoga practice that suits your lifestyle, so it's up to you how you want to approach the material. When you're ready to progress, in the next chapter, you'll learn about Bite-Size Yoga for your body!

* * * * *

100-Count Breath
REFLECTION NOTES

_____

_____

_____

_____

_____

_____

_____

_____

_____

_____

_____

_____

_____

_____

_____

_____

_____

_____

_____

_____

_____

_____

_____

_____

_____

_____

_____

_____

_____

_____

_____

_____

_____

_____

_____

_____

_____

_____

_____

_____

_____

_____

_____

_____

_____

_____

_____

_____

CHAPTER 6.

Technique #2
Bite-Size Yoga
for Your Body

Introduction

The Body in Yoga

Yoga that focuses on your body is called *asana*, or physical posture. In yoga, you stretch and strengthen your body through asana so that you can sit for long periods in meditation. If your body is hurting, you can't meditate.

An Achy Body is a Distracting Body

In today's world, we also spend a lot of time sitting, just not for meditation.

You sit at a desk or a table to work. You may also curl up on the couch for hours or have a long commute around town. As you sit, your shoulders start hunching, your neck curves down towards your phone or computer, and your legs and hips stiffen from immobility.

When you've sat for too long, your body starts to ache. Over time this ache can turn into chronic pain, distracting or even preventing you from completing the task at hand. Then, it becomes hard to relax because, when you do eventually unplug from your project, you finally feel all the pain you've been ignoring.

Why Should You Care?

Being in physical pain may also intensify emotional pain.

Back when my panic attacks were frequent, I noticed that my anxiety was more likely to escalate if I was already feeling physical discomfort. As the tension in my body grew, I had more difficulty breathing, eventually resulting in a panic attack.

But the mind-body connection is powerful. It can be used to your advantage if you make it work for you, rather than against you.

To help alleviate my anxiety, around 2010, I looked for my first yoga regular routine. My chosen yoga practice was a 20-minute video from a company called "Yoga Skool" that I did each morning in my living room. Definitely not formal training. Yet, this practice improved my overall level of anxiety so much that I woke up early every morning for the next two years just to fit it in before work.

When your body feels strong and secure, you mentally feel strong and secure, which has an immediate positive impact on your life!

Yoga Helps You Move

Because asana is the most commonly taught yoga practice, you may (or may not) be aware that there are many different ways to do yoga postures.

For example:

- You can hold postures to build strength.

- You can hold postures to increase flexibility.

- You can move quickly at a rate of one posture per breath.

- You can rest for long periods in restorative postures.

While your physique may change as a side-effect of your asana practice, this is not the goal of yoga asana. By listening and responding to the needs of your body with appropriate movement, you become more confident and grounded in your body, allowing you to feel calmer and work more efficiently. And with just a few poses sprinkled throughout your day, you can improve your physical and mental state with Bite-Size Yoga for your body.

Anyone Can Move

You don't need to be in peak physical condition to practice yoga for your body. You can start doing yoga postures with whatever physical limitations or injuries you have as long as you appropriately modify them to suit your range of motion.

Take my dad, for example. Clumsiness runs in our family. As he got older, he started having more accidents, injuring his shoulders and feet. These injuries took a lot longer to heal than years before. I knew a modified yoga practice could help him recover mobility faster, but I didn't know how to safely make adjustments for him. This was one of the reasons I wanted to become a yoga teacher.

Then, the day after my yoga teacher training ended, I started working with my dad on a personal yoga practice. I wanted to craft for him a daily practice that would be short enough that he couldn't make an excuse not to do it and one that was tailored to his physical goals and limitations.

As I taught it to him, we used nontraditional props and locations, like the kitchen table, to help modify poses for optimal strength-building and proper form. I even drew up all the sequences with stick figures and notes so that he could take his practice with him wherever he goes!

So, you, too, can relieve aches and build strength with a Bite-Size Yoga practice, no matter your fitness level. A healthy body will help you cultivate a healthy mind and spirit, and this next technique will help you get started!

* * *

Technique #2 The Desk Warrior

In Bite-Size Yoga, all you need is a few proper postures to soothe tensions as they start to accumulate during the day.

If you sit for most of your day, then you should get up and move around at least once every hour. While taking a quick walk is an excellent way to get your blood flowing, walking doesn't provide relief to as many muscular-skeletal systems as yoga does. In a single yoga pose, you might engage your feet, legs, hips, spine, neck, and arms!

Even if you're already on your feet all day, taking Bite-Size Yoga breaks helps to alleviate tensions that are building from repetitive stress and stiffness before they become chronic issues.

This next technique I call the desk warrior because it is a warrior pose you can easily do while at your desk without attracting too much attention. Any table-height object, countertop, or even just a wall will do as a natural prop you might find in your environment.

By using a desk or prop, you're able to build more strength and stability with proper form. Then, if you do want to practice away from your accessory or on your mat, your body will snap more firmly and securely into the right position.

When to Use:

Use this technique when your body starts getting a little achy, and you find yourself unconsciously stretching. It'll be a lot more efficient to take a conscious stretch break with Bite-Size Yoga than lose time and focus with a lot of shallow involuntary stretches as you work.

Instructions:

A video demonstration of this technique is available under the Free Book Bonuses at www.beautifulsoulnicole.com/bite-size-yoga.

Step 1. Make Space

Stand in front of your desk (or some kind of tabletop or wall). Clear the space a few feet behind you.

Step 2. Starting Stance

About a foot back from your table, stand with your feet hips width apart and parallel.

Place your hands on the table for support.

Level and square your hips to the table by tensing the muscles of your thighs.

Step 3. Warrior Feet

Step back with your right foot at least a foot or two. Pivot the toes on your right foot so that they point towards two o'clock or about 30 degrees right from the center.

Straighten your right leg, if you can. Keep your hips as level and square as you can without tweaking the back knee. *Pivot your toes back towards parallel or stop if you feel too much discomfort.*

Step 4. Activate Your Legs

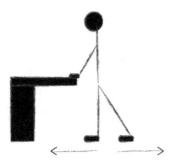

Now it's time to work the legs! Imagine that you're trying to tear the carpet or mat beneath you apart by driving your front foot forward and your back foot back. Continue to engage the thighs to keep the hips level and square.

You can control this internally created resistance to build strength and stamina, depending on how hard you press your feet into the ground while drawing your thighs together.

Step 5. Activate Your Core

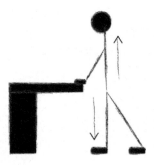

With your hands on the table for balance, lengthen your spine by lifting with your heart or stand tall like there is a string pulling from the crown of your head.

Think of your body as a toy finger trap. When you press your feet down and lift your heart up, the muscles of your core tighten and engage, like the finger trap. This supports your spine and creates stability.

Step 6. Lunge into Your Warrior

Once you feel stable and secure, bend your front left leg so that your left knee stacks over your left ankle. *Make sure you can still see your left toes to check that your knee hasn't gone too far.*

Continue to keep the back foot rooted and square the hips forward by tensing the thighs.

Step 7. Focus on a Point in Front of You

With your body stable, find a focal point either on the wall in front of you or at the tip of your nose, if it doesn't make you dizzy!

Step 8. Breathe!

With each inhale, press down into your feet and lengthen your spine up. With each exhale, soften and relax more deeply into your pose.

Place your hands wherever is most comfortable or leave them on the surface in front of you.

Step 9. Come Out of the Pose

Once you feel focused and ready to come out of this warrior pose, simply step the back leg forward, coming back into the first standing posture and shake out any engaged muscles to release tension.

Step 10. Switch Sides

When you're ready, start back at step one from the neutral standing stance and step back with the left foot. Repeat on the left side through step nine.

Your Turn

Practice makes progress. If you want to replace your current coping habits with new skills, then you need to practice. The more you practice a new technique, the more quickly you'll be able to remember it when you're stressed and need it most.

Pro Tip

Once you're comfortable with the structure of the pose, move your focus to your breath. You can even start the counting breath once you are in the pose for about 10 respirations on each side. By integrating your breath and body awareness, you pull your attention away from any external distractions so you can fully reset your focus and energy.

What's Next?

You can either:

1. Take a few days to fully explore this technique (reflecting on your experiences in the notes space provided on the next few pages), or

2. Review all the exercises at once and just play with them as you go.

You are building a Bite-Size Yoga practice that suits your lifestyle, so it's up to you how you want to approach the material. When you're ready to progress, in the next chapter, you'll learn about Bite-Size Yoga for your voice!

* * * * *

Desk Warrior
REFLECTION NOTES

_____

_____

_____

_____

_____

_____

_____

_____

_____

_____

_____

_____

_____

_____

_____

_____

_____

_____

_____

_____

_____

_____

_____

_____

_____

_____

_____

_____

_____

_____

_____

_____

_____

_____

_____

_____

_____

_____

_____

_____

_____

_____

_____

_____

_____

_____

_____

CHAPTER 7.

Technique #3
Bite-Size Yoga
for Your Voice

Introduction

The Voice in Yoga

One yoga practice that uses your voice is *mantra*, the chanting of specific Sanskrit words or phrases. Mantra means "mind tool" because these phrases focus the mind on healing sound vibrations rather than unproductive or runaway thoughts.

Negative Thoughts Paralyze Productivity

Your actions start as ideas or thoughts. But if your thoughts are caught in a broken record of "I can't do this. I'm not good enough," then you may be paralyzed from taking any action at all.

Why Should You Care?

Negative thoughts distract you from living a life you love.

In addition to physical symptoms, I can tell my anxiety is rising when my thoughts become a broken record of negativity.

For example, when I'm tired, it's tough to edit my writing. I get mad at all the unclear language in front of me as I struggle with simplifying it. With each wordy paragraph, I hear an internal monologue of, "You suck. Why are you doing this? You should never have started writing in the first place."

As I try to push through the negativity, the voices become more detailed. "Think of all the time and money you've wasted. What a wash. Give up and do something else." Ugh, it's terrible.

Each negative thought feeds the next as I become more hopeless. Eventually, I curl up in a ball under my blanket, paralyzed by my mental rant. I know this is not the headspace for making important decisions or changes, so I just wait it out and my day is lost.

The key to avoiding this scenario is to shut down those negative thoughts before they start swirling and taking a life of their own. I do this with mantra.

Yoga Helps You Silence Negative Thoughts with Mantra

When you chant a mantra, you produce sound.

Producing sound is a very physical activity. Air travels out of your lungs as you exhale and passes over your engaged vocal cords to create a sound vibration. You may even feel a tingling sensation through your face and nose as the sound is released. Then, those vibrations are picked up by your ears and registered back into your brain as sound waves.

Chanting mantra focuses your attention in the present moment. You can only hear the mantra for as long as you are making the sound with your body and breath. Once your breathing stops, the sound is gone. To hear the mantra again, you have to wait until the next repetition with the next breath. After five to 10 minutes of chanting mantra, your attention becomes entirely focused in the present moment. Whatever thoughts were happening before your mantra meditation are just a memory.

In yoga, the vibrations of the Sanskrit language are believed to have healing properties, and the mantras are chanted in multiples of 108. But you don't have to believe in sound healing to benefit from a mantra practice. Chant anything 108 times (or for at least five minutes), and you'll have drowned out whatever thoughts were distracting you from before.

Anyone Can Chant

At my old yoga studio in Michigan, I used to lead mantra chanting as well as singing mantra during the resting pose at the end of asana classes to encourage relaxation.

One day, before class, the studio manager had her children with her, ages two and four, so they could play in the kid's room while she took care of the studio. It was the two-year-old's birthday, and she was a little fussy.

The manager asked if I could sing with the kids. So, the manager, her four-year-old, and I sat in the studio with my *harmonium*, an Indian folk instrument. The two-year-old was having a moment, so she didn't want to come in.

I started singing and playing a simple melody with the mantra *om, shanti, om,* which is a mantra for peace. The manager sang along and encouraged her four-year-old daughter to sing with her. Suddenly, the daughter left the room. She wanted to bring in her younger sister, too. Soon both children were cuddled on their mother as we all sang together *om, shanti, om.*

The next week, the manager thanked me for introducing the mantra song to her children. She told me her older daughter started singing the younger one to sleep with it. My heart melted on the spot.

If mantra can quell the ups and downs of early childhood, imagine what it can do for you!

* * *

Technique #3 Om Shanti, Shanti, Shanti

For this next technique, I want you to try chanting a Sanskrit mantra.

Even if you aren't in a situation where you can easily chant a mantra out loud (although you may clear out an aisle on the bus for yourself if that's your goal), you can also chant mantra silently. Chanting or singing silently in your head is just as effective at drawing your focus inwards and experiencing the healing vibrations internally.

And while 108 rounds of a mantra are optimal, if you don't have a recording to follow along with or a mala necklace to count the rounds on, just set a timer for five to 10 minutes to create an immersive internal experience with your mantra.

The mantra in this technique is *om shanti, shanti, shanti*.

Om is a syllable that invokes the energy of the universe. It is grounding and centering. Most mantras start with or incorporate *om.* Also, you can just chant *om* by itself if you can't remember anything else.

Shanti means peace. When you say it three times, you are sending peace out in all directions, starting with yourself and expanding outward. It can be easier to hold the intention of shutting down negative thoughts when you know you are replacing them with feelings of peace.

When to Use:

Use this mantra when you find yourself caught in a cycle of disturbing thoughts. It will give you a chance to stop the automatic thought pattern, so you can reset and think more clearly and with intention.

Instructions:

If you are worried about chanting precisely 108 rounds of the mantra, download this mantra meditation MP3 from the Free Book Bonuses at www.beautifulsoulnicole.com/bite-size-yoga and just chant along!

Step 1. Find a Seat

Find a comfortable seat with a long straight spine.

Step 2. Set an Intention

Set an intention, "I wish to consciously let go of stress, anger, etc."

Step 3. Chant

Chant the mantra *om shanti, shanti, shanti* (silently or out loud) for 108 rounds or for five to 10 minutes. Try to be fully present with the mantra and the sounds you are creating as you chant.

Step 4. Breathe

When you are done, take a few deep breaths. Allow yourself to be in the present moment with the new state of calm you've created.

* * *

Your Turn

Practice makes progress. If you want to replace your current coping habits with new skills, then you need to practice. The more you practice a new technique, the more quickly you'll be able to remember it when you're stressed and need it most.

Pro Tip

While each mantra has a meaning, it's more effective to identify what that mantra means to you based on how you feel. This way, you develop a personal relationship with each mantra that you try and will intuitively know which one will serve you best at any particular moment.

If you haven't already, go to the Free Book Bonuses at www.beautifulsoulnicole.com/bite-size-yoga to download the MP3 recording of this mantra meditation and save it to your mobile device. That way, whenever you have a break and want to meditate, it's as simple as pressing play!

What's Next?

You can either:

1. Take a few days to fully explore this technique (reflecting on your experiences in the notes space provided on the next few pages), or

2. Review all the exercises at once and just play with them as you go.

You are building a Bite-Size Yoga practice that suits your lifestyle, so it's up to you how you want to approach the material. When you're ready to progress, in the next chapter, you'll learn about Bite-Size Yoga for your mind!

* * * * *

Om, Shanti, Shanti, Shanti
REFLECTION NOTES

_____

_____

_____

_____

_____

_____

_____

_____

_____

_____

_____

_____

_____

_____

_____

_____

_____

_____

_____

_____

_____

_____

_____

_____

_____

_____

_____

_____

_____

_____

_____

_____

_____

_____

_____

_____

_____

_____

_____

_____

_____

_____

_____

_____

_____

_____

_____

CHAPTER 8.

Technique #4 Bite-Size Yoga for Your Mind

Introduction

The Mind in Yoga

Yoga that focuses on cultivating your mind is called *jnana yoga*, or the study of philosophy. Just as you need steady breath and a strong body to practice yoga, you also need a healthy mind.

While you can use a mantra to stop cycles of negative thoughts, eventually you will need to replace the old beliefs that led to those cycles with more uplifting ones. This is where jnana yoga comes in.

An Invisible Enemy

In the last chapter, we looked at how negative thought loops can paralyze clear decision-making and productive action. But what about thoughts that don't loop?

A negative subconscious belief, such as you are not good enough or worthy of love, is a silent killer. It can poison your choices and actions. This belief took hold because it was fed to you at some point. Then, your subconscious continued to collect information to reinforce that belief.

If you want to make better choices more efficiently, you need to update the beliefs that are holding you back. But how do you modify an idea that is hiding in your subconscious?

Honestly, I'm not sure. But what you can do is feed yourself new beliefs and plant the seeds for new subconscious patterns that, with the proper nurturing, will take root.

Why You Should Care?

Your beliefs affect how you move through life.

After years of anxiety and alcoholism, I believed that there was fundamentally something wrong with me. I kept trying to do things that "normal people" do, like show up for work every day or take care of my apartment. When I couldn't consistently meet even just the basics of being a functional adult, I believed I was broken.

I went through humiliating patterns of working and quitting and working and quitting. I stopped trusting my decision-making abilities. And even though the negative self-talk wasn't continually cycling through my head, it was still underlying every choice I made throughout the day. I hit a personal rock bottom. I knew I needed a better solution because I didn't see much of a point in living like this.

So, I went to Peru. I spent three weeks in the jungles of the Amazon with a small group of Americans and three local shamans. We stayed in a village, eight hours by boat from the nearest city and the shamans led us through five ayahuasca ceremonies (a psychedelic plant medicine used in shamanic rituals). This was my self-intervention.

Through these ceremonies, my old toxic beliefs were shattered and replaced with compassion and purpose. Instead of thinking I was broken, I saw the changes I kept making in my career path as stepping stones to something greater and was encouraged not to give up. Within a few weeks of returning home, I was just done with alcohol and quickly became sober. I knew it would still take work to change my old patterns of anxiety, but, with new clarity, I sought professional help to fill in the gaps.

Not everyone wants to or has the chance to work with plant medicine led by shamans. But part of what drew me to yoga is that the philosophy described by yogic sages matches the experiences I had through plant medicine.

And with jnana yoga, I can continue to reinforce these positive beliefs by feeding my mind with healthy thoughts.

Yoga Helps You Think

Judeo-Christian traditions have the 10 commandments, Buddhism has the eightfold path, and yogic philosophy has the eight limbs of yoga. The eight limbs of yoga include not just the physical practices of yoga but also philosophical guidance for "right living." The details of right living are described in the *yamas* (how not to live) and *niyamas* (how to live).

The *yamas* tell you **not** to practice:

- Violence,

- Lying,

- Stealing,

- Marital Infidelity,

- Or Greed.

Which means you **should** be practicing:

- Nonviolence,

- Honesty,

- Integrity,

- Loyalty,

- And Non-Possessiveness.

The *niyamas* tell you to **practice**:

- Purity of Mind, Body, and Spirit,

- Contentment,

- Self-Discipline,

- Self-Reflection,

- And Reflection on Supreme Consciousness.

These seem pretty standard across world spiritual traditions, so there should be no surprises here. But applying yogic philosophy to your life, in a way that supports your day-to-day experience, is how you bridge the gap from theoretical principles to practical tools.

Anyone Can Develop New Beliefs

Let's take the yogic value of nonviolence. You may not consider yourself a violent person on the outside, but what about your thoughts? Do you sometimes think or say things that are harmful to yourself or others?

When students first come to my yoga classes, they often have so many negative things to say about themselves. And it's not just what they say, but how they say it. For example, they say they're not as flexible or in as good of shape as they used to be. Now, these could be objective statements or just metrics they want to see improvement on. But these statements are often delivered with tones of shame or embarrassment. Like there is something wrong with not being flexible or your body changing over time.

The students who speak of themselves in this way are generally the most sensitive to making, what they perceive to be, mistakes in class and will be too embarrassed to return if they think they're not good enough. These negative beliefs are harmful because they prevent self-improving action.

In class, I try to steer my students away from self-judgmental thinking, in particular, when we work on poses that have a left-side and right-side version. While yoga seeks balance, everyone has a side that is stronger or weaker than the other. You may be able to balance easily on your right foot in tree pose, but then quickly wobble or fall over when attempting it on the left. Rather than assign one leg as good or bad, I encourage my students to think of their two sides as children. Each has with their own strengths and weaknesses, and you love them equally.

When you train your mind to be more compassionate with your body, those new patterns of thinking lead you to becoming more compassionate with yourself, as well as others. Therefore, you are instilling and practicing new nonviolent beliefs!

* * *

Technique #4 You Are Enough

To perform Bite-Size Yoga for your mind, you first need to catch the thoughts that are harmful to you and replace them with ones that lift you up.

"You are enough" is an example of a nonviolent thought, because it counters any self-deprecating beliefs of being less-than or unworthy so that you have the confidence to make decisions and actions that are in your best interest.

This technique takes only two minutes or less per day, so there's no reason not to fit it into your routine!

When to Use:

Do **part one** of this technique in the morning while you're getting ready for the day and have access to a mirror. Then do **part two** during the day whenever you catch yourself using negative self-talk.

Instructions:

Part 1

In the morning

Step 1. Find Your Reflection

Look at yourself in a mirror (or selfie-cam or whatever reflective surface is available to you).

Step 2. Speak to Your Subconscious

Look yourself in the eyes and say, **"You are enough."** Even if you don't consider yourself a touchy-feely person, just go with it.

Step 3. Connect for a Minute

Repeat step two for at least one minute or longer. Really connect with your own soul the way you would talk to a dear friend.

It's okay if you have an emotional release or cry. You are trying to access and heal your subconscious self.

Part 2

Throughout the day

Step 1. Catch Negative Self-Talk

As you go about your day, catch yourself when you think any implication of "You're not good enough."

Step 2. Replace It with the New Belief

When you do, place your hand over your heart, close your eyes, and replace the negative thought by saying to yourself, **"I am enough,"** at least three times.

* * *

Your Turn

Practice makes progress. If you want to replace your current coping habits with new skills, then you need to practice. The more you practice a new technique, the more quickly you'll be able to remember it when you're stressed and need it most.

Pro Tip

Because you are trying to change buried subconscious beliefs, the more consistently you do this technique throughout your day, the more success you'll have instilling the new nonviolent belief within yourself. And this technique only takes seconds once you get the hang of it!

If your mind is already spinning out-of-control, start with a mantra technique to clear your mind. Otherwise, nothing will stick. Then you can introduce the new belief with the practice above.

What's Next?

You can either:

1. Take a few days to fully explore this technique (reflecting on your experiences in the notes space provided on the next few pages), or

2. Review all the exercises at once and just play with them as you go.

You are building a Bite-Size Yoga practice that suits your lifestyle, so it's up to you how you want to approach the material. When you're ready to progress, in the next chapter, you'll learn about Bite-Size Yoga for your spirit!

* * * * *

You Are Enough
REFLECTION NOTES

_____

_____

_____

_____

_____

_____

_____

_____

_____

_____

_____

_____

_____

_____

_____

_____

_____

_____

_____

_____

_____

_____

_____

_____

_____

_____

_____

_____

_____

_____

_____

_____

CHAPTER 9.

Technique #5
Bite-Size Yoga
for Your Spirit

Introduction

The Spirit in Yoga

Yoga that focuses on your spirit is called *dhyana yoga*, or meditation. In yoga, your spirit is your higher consciousness. The point of this entire practice, using tools to calm your breath, body, voice, and mind, is so that you can connect with your spirit and live in complete alignment with your higher consciousness.

Not a tall order, right?

Accessing Your Inner Wisdom

When you connect with your spirit or higher consciousness, you can access your intuitive wisdom. You can receive and interpret subtle messages to help you along your path. And in yoga, to properly receive guidance from your highest self, you need a calm and clear channel.

If your life is full of distractions such as an aching body, erratic breathing, barrages of negative thoughts or beliefs, etc., you may not get the message or, even worse, it may be scrambled and misinterpreted.

Why Should You Care?

Only your truth will lead you along your most fulfilling path.

Growing up, I realized there were a lot of different points of view for how I should be and what I should do with my life:

- The media indicated that I should be thin, beautiful, and well-liked at all costs.

- The job market dictated I should have a resume full of prestigious education and experience, so I am never unemployed.

- My parents said I should follow a traditional career path to ensure conventional success.

- And yet my heart just wished to sing on Broadway!

My teen years were subsequently marked by 'people pleasing' and seeking external validation from those around me. I had an eating disorder, and I gave up my musical theater. Later, I went to an Ivy League college and studied international relations like a good social citizen. But when I graduated and entered the job market during the recession at the end of 2009, none of it mattered.

There were no jobs, not even for prestigious degrees, and I couldn't sing anymore because I had stopped training. The position I did end up getting paid less than what I could have made as a struggling actress waiting tables. Listening to everyone's voice, but my own left me confused and depressed, which led to my anxiety disorder and alcoholism.

The biggest issue I had, through all those significant decision-making years, was figuring out how to quiet everyone else's desires so that I could hear my own intuitively guided voice.

And how do you tune out the noise, so you can hear your inner guidance?

Yoga Helps You Connect with Your Spirit

Yoga teaches you the practice of meditation to quiet all the distractions in your life, whether they come from within or outside of you. When all is quiet, your inner wisdom comes through. It's a tranquil and subtle experience. Everything just feels okay.

Sometimes you may even experience a body high or receive extraordinary information once you've relaxed into a meditative trance. Yoga philosophy acknowledges this kind of meditative extrasensory occurrence but warns against becoming attached to or distracted by it. It is a potential side-effect of the practice (like a muscular physique from asana) but should not be valued as a marker of success.

The goal of yoga is always just finding union with what is.

Anyone Can Connect with Their Spirit

Most people are very open to meditation when they have something to grieve. Whether you're grieving a loved one, the end of a relationship, or the conclusion of a phase of life, there is usually such a mass of emotions that need to be released that words alone aren't capable of processing it all.

My father is a veterinary oncologist, so I grew up with a lot of animals in my childhood. As an only child, they were the nearest thing to siblings I had. When I took my self-imposed anxiety leave from the corporate world, I wanted to get a therapy cat to help ease my depression.

I had scanned the adoption websites for weeks and frequented the cat adoption section of the pet store each time I went to the grocery store next door. One day, as I was passing by, the pet store employees were taking the cats out one-at-a-time for their daily exercise.

The first cat they took out was skittish and had more emotional scars than I did. The second cat though walked right up to me and flopped on her side to be petted.

I had been chosen.

She was a black, fluffy senior cat with a bit of an abandonment complex named Raven. She followed me around and stayed by my side as I moped around. She never judged me for drinking and always forgave me for leaving her alone while I was away at work. As I eventually attempted new jobs and new relationships, she was the one constant I always came home to.

As I prepared to move cross-country to Michigan with my partner at the time, I found out that she had rare bladder cancer and only had a few weeks to live. I spoiled her rotten and got a few more months with her, but it was evident when the time had come for her last day. My boyfriend and I stayed with her at the vet for the procedure and said our goodbyes from what had been three beautiful years with her.

As we sat on the couch back in our apartment after she was gone, we were beside ourselves with grief. My boyfriend asked me if there was anything he could do. I asked him to meditate with me to see if we could receive any messages from her. At the time, he was not one to meditate unless I requested him to do it with me, and this time, he lovingly obliged.

We sat and closed our eyes. I surrendered my grief and just listened for any echoes inside the deep caverns of my consciousness. Eventually, I heard, "There are more cats to be rescued." My then boyfriend, not a spiritual person, also received a message for him.

While periods of intense emotional drama can motivate profound change and truth-seeking, you don't have to wait for overwhelming circumstances to start a meditation practice. In fact, regularly releasing accumulated emotional tensions helps keep you clear-minded and confident in the daily decisions you are making.

* * *

Technique #5 Grounding Meditation

Meditation may seem intimidating, but a simple visualization meditation can provide enough imagery to be focusing as well as emotionally calming. This technique is a guided meditation that uses the imagery of grounding like a tree to let go of emotional tensions.

When to Use:

When you feel mentally foggy, or your judgment is clouded by emotions.

Instructions:

Because this is a guided meditation, you can either read through the whole meditation first and then do the visualization on your own or you can download the meditation in the Free Book Bonuses at <u>www.beautifulsoulnicole.com/bite-size-yoga</u> and visualize along with the recording.

Step 1. Find Your Seat

Sit in a chair with your feet planted on the ground, hands on your thighs palms up, and a long straight spine. Close your eyes.

Step 2. Focus Your Attention

Focus your attention in the center of your head, between your ears and behind the center of your eyebrows.

Step 3. Visualize Your Body

As if you are watching a movie screen projected between your eyebrows, visualize your body seated in a chair just like you are in real life.

Step 4. Call in Your Aura

Call in all your non-physical energy so that it forms a bubble or aura a foot or two around, above, and below your body.

Step 5. Connect to the Center of the Earth

From the base of your spine, imagine a beam of light, the width of your hips, shooting down and connecting you to the center of the earth like a grounding cord.

Step 6. Release Old Energy Down

Each time you exhale, release any heavy or negative energy from your aura down this grounding cord to the center of the earth to be recycled.

Step 7. Allow the Earth to Connect Back to You

From the center of the earth, imagine a tree trunk springing up around your grounding cord, connecting back up to your hips and aura.

Step 8. Allow the Earth to Connect to Your Feet

From this tree trunk grows two branches. They connect to the *chakras*, or wheels of energy, at the soles of your feet.

Step 9. Receive Fresh Energy from the Earth

As you inhale, you receive fresh, abundant earth energy as it travels through your feet, your ankles, your knees, and your hips, washing through your root chakra at the base of your spine.

Step 10. Release Any Extra Energy Back Down

As you exhale, release any excess earth energy back down your grounding cord, strengthening your connection to the earth.

Step 11. Notice Any Sensations or Messages

Take a few minutes to observe any sensations. Do you sense a color, feeling, or temperature associated with the flow of earth energy? Do any other thoughts, feelings, colors, or sensations come up as you focus on the energy being released? Are you yawning, twitching, or noticing any physical manifestations of the energy-releasing?

Step 12. Come Out of Your Meditation

When you feel complete for this session, allow your awareness to drop from your head down into your heart-center in your physical body. Begin to wiggle your fingers and toes, and gently flutter your eyes open. You can fold forward and touch the floor to release any extra energy.

* * *

Your Turn

Practice makes progress. If you want to replace your current coping habits with new skills, then you need to practice. The more you practice a new technique, the more quickly you'll be able to remember it when you're stressed and need it most.

Pro Tip

If you haven't already, go to the Free Book Bonuses at www.beautifulsoulnicole.com/bite-size-yoga to download the MP3 recording of this meditation or read the meditation script above out loud with a recorder and save it to your phone. That way, whenever you have a break and want to meditate, it's as simple as pressing play!

What's Next?

You can either:

1. Take a few days to fully explore this technique (reflecting on your experiences in the notes space provided on the next few pages), or

2. Review all the exercises at once and just play with them as you go.

You are building a Bite-Size Yoga practice that suits your lifestyle, so it's up to you how you want to approach the material.

* * * * *

Grounding Meditation
REFLECTION NOTES

_____

_____

_____

_____

_____

_____

_____

_____

_____

_____

_____

_____

_____

_____

_____

_____

_____

_____

_____

_____

_____

_____

_____

_____

_____

_____

_____

_____

_____

_____

_____

_____

_____

_____

_____

_____

_____

_____

_____

_____

_____

_____

_____

_____

_____

_____

_____

_____

* * * * *

Now that you've tried out these five Bite-Size Yoga techniques, how do you apply them to your day so that you get sweet relief while you're on-the-go?

In the next section, you'll learn the Bite-Size Yoga system that makes adding yoga to your day effortless and natural as well as some time savers for organizing your new toolkit of Bite-Size Yoga techniques.

* * * * *

Section 2. Bite-Size Review

Good golly Miss Molly! Look at all the Bite-Size Yoga techniques you've tried. Hopefully, some have resonated with you and you were able to download your MP3 meditations to make your practice even more convenient!

Let's take a moment to review what we've covered in this section:

1. You no longer have to choose between productivity and taking care of your health, thanks to Bite-Size Yoga.

2. With Bite-Size Yoga, you can enhance your workflow with single techniques that easily fit into your day.

3. You now have five Bite-Size Yoga techniques that you can use to refresh your energy, and refocus, quickly:

    a. The 100-Count Breath Pranayama (for your breath)

    b. The Desk Warrior Asana (for your body)

    c.   The Om Shanti, Shanti, Shanti Mantra (for your voice)

    d.   The You Are Enough Practice (for your mind)

    e.   The Grounding Meditation Visualization (for your spirit)

You've tried out a few exercises. Now what? How do you integrate your favorites seamlessly into your day so that they don't become just another forgotten self-help tool?

In the next section, we'll look at a simple schedule for taking these Bite-Size Yoga techniques from new tools to automatic habits, and of course, how to keep track of them all. Full speed ahead!

SECTION 3.

A Successful System

What makes Bite-Size Yoga more than just a collection of recycled yoga and meditation techniques? It's the implementation system behind it that effortlessly incorporates these exercises into your day so that they become automatic and your new go-to productivity habit!

By the end of this section, you'll be able to answer and reflect on these three questions:

1. What is the Bite-Size Yoga system for a consistent and healthy lifestyle?

2. What do you do with the knowledge you gain from yoga classes, workshops, and retreats so that you get the biggest bang for your buck?

3. How do you organize your growing collection of Bite-Size Yoga techniques so that you never have to waste time searching for forgotten exercises?

If you're ready to start seeing some real results in your work day, with easy routines you can actually stick to, then it's time to jump into the final section of this Bite-Size Yoga system!

CHAPTER 10.

The Bite-Size Yoga Meal Plan

Systematize Your Change

Give New Habits a Fighting Chance

After testing out several Bite-Size Yoga techniques and figuring out what works best for you, the next step is to commit to making those techniques automatic.

You've spent a lot of years working on your old coping techniques that feed the endless cycles of working and crashing. To give yourself a chance at manageable life-style changes, before you need drastic health intervention, you have to systematize the new techniques you've learned so that they become the new habit.

And the key to consistent results starts with consistent practice.

Why You Want a System

When I was doing my teacher training at a yoga *ashram*, or spiritual retreat center, in Colorado, I was surrounded by idyllic beauty and pure spiritual intention. Easy to relax in a place like this?

No way.

Like toxins rising to the surface, my head swirled with all the unresolved negative memories that I hadn't yet dealt with.

Before each class session, we chanted a mantra. It felt great at the moment and kept me focused for class, but in between sessions, the old thoughts and worries kept arising.

After a week of practicing mantra every day, several times a day, whenever my mind started to wander into negativity, I quickly switched to a mantra meditation to drown out those thoughts.

After three weeks of consistent practice, I found my mind going straight to mantras, even outside of class. I realized I had trained my brain to skip the negative thoughts all together! Of course, I still had problems to deal with, but I could choose when I wanted to address them without distracting from whatever task I was presently involved in.

But you don't have to seclude yourself in a yoga ashram for weeks to make your Bite-Size Yoga techniques an automatic habit. You just need a straightforward system that gives you results!

* * *

The Bite-Size Yoga Meal Plan

Taking your Bite-Size Yoga techniques from just tools you've tried once or twice to a system that gives you consistent results, supporting your health and productivity, is as easy as following a meal plan!

The Bite-Size Yoga Meal Plan is an intuitive system for a regular daily practice that reinforces new habits as well as integrate Bite-Size Yoga throughout your day for immediate relief.

There are only three parts to the Bite-Size Yoga Meal Plan:

1. Your Yoga Breakfast

2. Your Yoga Snacks

3. Your Yoga Dessert

And if you tried out the techniques in the format I outlined in the previous section, you'll already be familiar with this approach!

* * *

Your Yoga Breakfast

The key to a successful new habit is to make it automatic. The way your new pattern becomes automatic is by practicing it and reinforcing it when the pressure is off so that you can easily recall it when the pressure is on. The best time to do this is first thing in the morning, **your yoga breakfast**.

The Most Important Meal of the Day

You already know that breakfast is the most important meal of the day. While you sleep, you're fasting. When you wake up, you need to refuel your body with nutrients to give yourself a quick burst of energy and keep you full until your next meal.

Starting your day with Bite-Size Yoga lays the foundation for how the rest of your day will go. It draws your attention inward as you refresh your mind, body, and spirit. Additionally, you remind your brain to make your health a priority as you start on your daily checklists and projects.

With a yoga breakfast, you prime your mind to recall these exercises later in the day. By practicing each morning, you reinforce the neural pathways that take Bite-Size Yoga from a passing activity to an automatic reflex.

Two Types of Breakfast

There are two ways to approach your yoga breakfast, depending on how much time you have or want to put in:

1. **When you're short on time:** Focus on your favorite Bite-Size Yoga technique or the one you are currently learning.

2. **When you have time for a whole meal:** For a complete balanced yoga breakfast, do one exercise from all five of the Bite-Size Yoga flavors to fully wake up your breath, body, voice, mind, and spirit.

I recommend starting with just one of your favorite Bite-Size Yoga exercises to establish your yoga breakfast routine. This single practice may be all the yoga you need to feel fully satisfied in the morning and start your day on the right foot.

Then, once you reach the point where you wake up craving your morning yoga practice, because of the results it gives, you may find yourself wanting to do more. To expand your yoga breakfast, just add whatever next technique you're most drawn to at that moment.

This system isn't about drastic changes or doing yoga just for the sake of doing yoga. Keep your Bite-Size Yoga meals simple and relevant to your needs. This way, your practice can be flexible to the natural changes in your life and evolves with you.

* * *

Your Yoga Snacks

So, you've had your yoga breakfast. You're feeling full and even-keeled as you move about your day. Eventually, though, your energy will deplete, and you'll be hungry again. This is where you add in a single Bite-Size Yoga technique: **your yoga snack**.

Like a snack that ties you over until your next meal, you can choose the Bite-Size Yoga technique that will get you back to feeling your best most efficiently until you have more time to rest and renew:

1. **Feeling agitated?** Do a breath technique.

2. **Your body is stiff?** Do a body technique.

3. **Swirling thoughts?** Do a voice technique.

4. **Negative self-talk?** Do a mind technique.

5. **Feeling foggy?** Do a spirit technique.

These associations are just a format to get you started. Whatever technique you find yourself drawn to, or that you practiced that morning, is the best one for you. Don't overthink it. Just do yoga.

As long as you consciously take a break and give your Bite-Size Yoga snack your full attention, even if for just a few minutes, you will feel satiated. You'll also notice that with each repetition your experience with your Bite-Size Yoga techniques will evolve.

In time, your Bite-Size Yoga snacks will get more useful as you train your brain that this action is the signal for quick renewal, and it will cooperate faster. Yoga snacks are self-care on-the-go!

* * *

Your Yoga Dessert

With just your yoga breakfast and yoga snacks, you've got everything you need for living the Bite-Size Yoga life-style! But what about your yoga classes?

With the Bite-Size Yoga Meal Plan, yoga classes (once your only source of yogic nutrition) are now a delicious treat that you can indulge in whenever you have the time, or money, to invest in them.

What Are Yoga Desserts?

Yoga desserts are any yogic activity or education you get from events like classes, workshops, retreats, or even videos on the Internet. These kinds of experiences allow you to get creative with your yoga practice through new ideas and influences. And because your Bite-Size Yoga practice has given you a foundation in several styles of yoga, you can more effectively choose and remember different yoga activities that are most interesting to you.

How Do Yoga Classes Affect My Bite-Size Yoga Practice?

Since you have your own daily practice of Bite-Size Yoga, with yoga desserts, you can either:

1. Just relax and enjoy your time in yoga classes as a special treat,

2. Or mine your yoga classes, workshops, and retreats for new ideas to add to your Bite-Size Yoga Toolkit.

With Bite-Size Yoga, your yoga dessert benefits don't just end when a class is over. After your yoga class, workshop, or retreat, you can jot down any new ideas or techniques that resonated with you and add them to your Bite-Size Yoga Toolkit.

These days, every yoga class is different. Each instructor brings his or her own point-of-view and experiences to their environment. There are even fusions of yoga with other activities such as dance, shamanism, and sports, to name a few.

While some may lament the authenticity of these new innovations, yogic philosophy states that the tools it provides aren't the only means of achieving *yoga* or spiritual oneness. If other exercises bring you healthfully into union with your mind, body, and spirit, then you are practicing yoga. This means there is no wrong way to do yoga as long as it serves you.

Because you now have a context for better relating to other yogic experiences with Bite-Size Yoga, you can get the best return on your investment in yoga classes, workshops, and retreats because you can record your favorite lessons and add them to your toolkit of Bite-Size Yoga exercises!

A Growing List

Now that you've reached the point of trying new techniques, how will you keep track of your favorites so that you can recall them quickly and easily? In the next chapter, we'll look at a fast and simple system to organize your Bite-Size Yoga techniques into an actual toolkit so that you don't have to waste time or energy, trying to hunt down old exercises.

* * * * *

Chapter 10. Bite-Size Review

1. Take your Bite-Size Yoga practice from a solution you've dabbled with to a system of automatic habits with the Bite-Size Yoga Meal Plan.

2. The best way to start your day is with a healthy yoga breakfast of your favorite Bite-Size Yoga technique (or techniques).

3. Then use yoga snacks, the individual bite-size techniques, throughout your day to stay full and refreshed while you're on-the-go.

4. Enjoy your yoga classes, workshops, and re-treats as your unique yoga desserts, if and when you have time for them.

5. Then, mine these yoga classes, and different yoga experiences, for new techniques that reso-nate with you to add more variety and exercises to your Bite-Size Yoga Toolkit.

CHAPTER 11.

Your Bite-Size Yoga Toolkit

Organize Your Bite-Size Yoga Techniques

Life Happens

At this point, you've tried a few techniques and have an idea of what works for you. You don't have a lot of time and just plan on sticking to a single exercise. Why would you write it down? The point is to make it automatic, right?

But let's face it, life happens.

Especially while you're just starting out with your Bite-Size Yoga practice, things may come up, and you miss a day or two. Then one day, you're in the middle of a crash or wholly frustrated by the swirling thoughts and emotions running through your head. You remember that you can do a quick yoga practice to try to get back to a rested state. But what was that practice again?

Managing Your Growing Practice

Alternatively, what if your Bite-Size Yoga serves you so well that you can't keep track of all the cool techniques you've tried? Your friends and family admire your new level of well-being and ask you how you got started. You want to share with them all your notes, but you don't have any!

You can only remember the exercises you're currently doing. When those practices feel stale, you want to switch them up with the ones you learned a few months before. However, you'd have to take the time to find the instructions for those techniques and then, relearn them all over again.

If you just had some kind of Bite-Size Yoga folder for quick reference, you wouldn't have to reinvest your time looking for the old techniques you've already learned!

* * *

Create a Bite-Size Yoga Toolkit

Use What's Best, But Save the Rest

In Section 2, you learned how the different Bite-Size Yoga techniques make up what I call your Bite-Size Yoga Toolkit. Over time, you may be drawn more or less to various tools. But if you keep track of all the tools you've tried, you'll never have to reinvest that time researching or relearning the Bite-Size Yoga techniques that you haven't used in a while.

Make your Bite-Size Yoga Toolkit an actual folder for storing all your techniques. Then, your exercises will always be easily accessible when you need them most!

A DIY Toolkit

To create your Bite-Size Yoga Toolkit:

1. Create a folder (digitally or physically) and label it "Bite-Size Yoga Toolkit."

2. Take a screenshot, copy and paste, or write up the current Bite-Size Yoga exercise you're learning and store it in your folder.

That's it!

And if you love organizational systems as much as I do, you can also label each technique based on which flavor of yoga it falls under (breath, body, voice, mind, or spirit) by creating subfolders in your toolkit. That way, when you're looking for Bite-Size Yoga techniques for just your breath, for example, you can quickly scan through all the breathing exercises you've tried without wasting any time.

A Done-For-You Toolkit

Go to www.beautifulsoulnicole.com/bite-size-yoga and access the **Bite-Size Yoga Free Book Bonuses** course to download your pre-made digital toolkit of all the Bite-Size Yoga exercises covered in this book.

Then, you can either save the digital toolkit to your computer or print out the files to store them in a physical folder for easy reference.

* * *

Now's the Time

You've got the techniques. You've got the system. Now you just need to take action! In the final chapter, we'll wrap up the next steps you need to take to transform Bite-Size Yoga from just a theory to your new reality.

* * * * *

Chapter 11. Bite-Size Review

1. Life happens, and you may forget techniques that you've already invested time in learning.

2. Create a Bite-Size Yoga Toolkit folder to easily save your exercises for quick reference. Then, you won't waste time trying to find or relearn techniques that you've already tried.

3. If you don't want to create your own toolkit, download a pre-made folder for all of the exercises found in this book under the **Bite-Size Yoga Free Book Bonuses** online course at www.beautifulsoulnicole.com/bite-size-yoga.

Section 3. Bite-Size Review

Hooray! Those systems for when to practice and how to organize your growing collection of Bite-Size Yoga exercises weren't so painless and, dare I say, doable. Why not give it a try? Let's take a moment to review what we covered in this section:

1. Go from experimentation to systemization by automating your new habits with the Bite-Size Yoga Meal Plan.

2. Enjoy your yoga classes, workshops, and retreats as special treats. Mine them for inspiration for your daily routine. You no longer need to rely on them as the only source of your regular yoga practice.

3. Easily organize your new techniques into your Bite-Size Yoga Toolkit so that you never waste time looking for, or relearning, techniques that you've already tried.

Is it really time to wrap things up? Let's put this practical methodology into action. Are you pumped for your new Bite-Size Yoga routine? Let's review and cover your next steps for adding Bite-Size Yoga to your life for long-term health and productivity!

CONCLUSION

Don't Burn Out Creating the Life You Love

You want to rock at your career, be a great parent and partner, and still be healthy enough to tackle your retirement bucket list after all the decades of work you've put in. But if you keep pushing yourself until you crash all the time, you'll burn out your future health, happiness, and well-being long before you get a chance to enjoy it.

And while you may not be able to change the responsibilities you currently have; you can always change the way you go about getting them done.

Find Balance with Bite-Size Yoga

The key to a healthy workflow is to replace your current work-crash cycle with a work-rest cycle that you can do anywhere and in a short amount of time so that you can bounce back from stress quickly and healthily.

With Bite-Size Yoga, you can insert that much-needed centering and refreshment into your routine. Then you not only feel more rested during the day, but your work-flow also becomes more productive and consistent.

* * *

What's Next?

You've just invested precious hours learning about which lifestyle choices cause you to burn out and how Bite-Size Yoga can help you to balance your day with rest and productivity. Don't let this be just another book that you finish and forget about. Put these lessons into action!

A Bite-Size Game Plan for Success

Here's what you need to do to start benefiting from Bite-Size Yoga today:

1. Pick the **Bite-Size Yoga technique** you're most interested in from Section 2 for either your breath, body, voice, mind, or spirit.

2. Copy or screenshot it over to a folder where you'll be able to easily access it and add notes. This will be your **Bite-Size Yoga Toolkit**.

3. Commit to the **Bite-Size Yoga Meal Plan** for the next week. This includes:

   a. **Your Yoga Breakfast**: Practice your chosen technique each morning for the next week.

   b. **Your Yoga Snacks:** During the day, as your energy starts to wane, rather than a coffee, cookie, or smoke break, try out your Bite-Size Yoga technique.

4. At the end of the week, take some notes to **reflect on your Bite-Size Yoga practice**:

   a. How do you feel after doing the technique for a week?

   b. How did your experience change throughout the week?

   c. Were you able to practice your technique first thing in the morning as well as throughout the day?

   d. Did this technique benefit you enough that you'd like to keep using it, or would you prefer to move on to something else?

5. **Save your reflection notes** with the matching technique in your Bite-Size Yoga Toolkit folder so that you know which exercise to use when you want to recreate those feelings.

6. **Make the good ones automatic**. If you enjoyed this technique, and you'd like to focus on it for a while, integrate it more deeply into your routine by continuing with your Bite-Size Yoga Meal Plan until it becomes second nature. Then, you can choose whether to stick with just the one or add another technique by repeating the above process.

7. **Keep exploring**. If the first technique didn't resonate with you, try another one from a different flavor of yoga until you discover what works best for you!

There's no right or wrong when realizing the tools that provide you with health *and* sustainable productivity. You may experience some trial-and-error as you look for the best solutions, but hopefully, this book has made your self-development process more streamlined and has saved you some time along the way.

* * *

Inspire Others

Lead the example you want to see in the world. Revolutionize your workflow with Bite-Size Yoga and inspire your friends and family to find a healthier way to manage their daily responsibilities and cultivate self-care.

If you have any other questions or feedback on how to make Bite-Size Yoga a part of your daily routine, you can always reach me at www.beautifulsoulnicole.com/contact.

I wish you success in your Bite-Size Yoga adventures!

RESOURCES

Congratulations!

I hope you enjoyed this introduction to Bite-Size Yoga and are hungry for more!

Free Book Bonuses

Written instructions are helpful, but video demonstrations are always better!

Go to www.beautifulsoulnicole.com/bite-size-yoga to access the **Bite-Size Yoga Free Book Bonuses** course. Watch video demonstrations and download MP3s and PDFs for all the techniques taught in this book.

5-Week Online Course

Using the same link, check out the **5-Week Bite-Size Yoga Boot Camp** online course. In this comprehensive video course, with the dedication of a simple daily schedule, you'll incrementally add five new Bite-Size Yoga techniques to your day for lasting stress and energy management!

* * *

Reach Out

Do you have any other questions or want to reach out? Message me at <u>www.beautifulsoulnicole.com/contact</u>.

* * * * *

Plant Good Karma

If you haven't already, I would really appreciate your honest feedback in an online review!

Also, please share this book, and its ideas, with any friends or family members you think it may help.

Thank you for trying Bite-Size Yoga!

* * * * * * *

ABOUT THE AUTHOR

Nicole Page is a certified yoga instructor, kirtan singer, energy healer, and performance artist. Her healing journey started after hitting rock bottom with alcoholism, addiction, and anxiety. This led her to study yoga, arts, and shamanism in North and South America. Now, she hopes to empower others to access their own capacity for intuitive self-healing by providing simple tools and techniques that anyone can easily integrate into his or her everyday life.

Nicole has a B.A. from Brown University and an M.A. from the University of Washington, Seattle, in Russian and Slavic Linguistics. She is a jack-of-all-trades, having worked in major corporations and software development as well as in small businesses, academia, and now as an entrepreneur, artist, and yoga teacher. Through these experiences, Nicole has connected with global communities and seen the detrimental effects of stress and discontentment in many segments of society. She believes a happier and healthier way of life is accessible to all people and that the journey begins by developing an honest and heart-centered connection with oneself.

You can follow her adventures, healing arts, and offerings at www.beautifulsoulnicole.com.

Made in the USA
Middletown, DE
11 February 2021

33530788R00109